Entrepreneurial
Finance
A Definitive Guide

New Teaching Resources for Management in a Globalised World

Print ISSN: 2661-4774
Online ISSN: 2661 4782

Series Editor: Professor Léo-Paul Dana

The classic economic view of internationalisation was based on the theory of competitive advantage, and over the years, internationalisation was seen in various lights, as an expansion option. With the reduction of trade barriers, however, many local small enterprises face major international competitors in formerly protected domestic markets. Today, competitiveness in the global marketplace is no longer an option; it has become a necessity as the acceleration towards globalisation offers unprecedented challenges and opportunities.

This book series will bring together textbooks, monographs, edited collections and handbooks useful to postgraduates and researchers in the age of globalisation. Relevant topics include, but are not limited to: research methods, culture, entrepreneurship, globalisation, immigration, migrants, public policy, self-employment, sustainability, technological advances, emerging markets, demographic shifts, and innovation.

Published:

Resources for
Management
and
Globalisation
Volume 2

Entrepreneurial Finance
A Definitive Guide

Francesca Tenca
Vincenzo Butticè
Massimo Gaetano Colombo
Annalisa Croce
Massimiliano Guerini
Giancarlo Giudici
Politecnico di Milano, Italy

World Scientific

NEW JERSEY · LONDON · SINGAPORE · BEIJING · SHANGHAI · HONG KONG · TAIPEI · CHENNAI · TOKYO

Published by

World Scientific Publishing Co. Pte. Ltd.

5 Toh Tuck Link, Singapore 596224

USA office: 27 Warren Street, Suite 401-402, Hackensack, NJ 07601

UK office: 57 Shelton Street, Covent Garden, London WC2H 9HE

Library of Congress Cataloging-in-Publication Data
Names: Tenca, Francesca, author.
Title: Entrepreneurial finance : a definitive guide / Francesca Tenca, Vincenzo Butticè,
    Massimo Gaetano Colombo, Annalisa Croce, Massimiliano Guerini,
    Giancarlo Giudici (Politecnico di Milano, Italy).
Description: USA : World Scientific, 2020. | Series: New teaching resources for management in a
    globalised world, 2661-4774 ; vol. 2 | Includes bibliographical references and index.
Identifiers: LCCN 2020034087 (print) | LCCN 2020034088 (ebook) |
    ISBN 9789811221972 (hardcover) | ISBN 9789811221989 (ebook) |
    ISBN 9789811221996 (ebook other)
Subjects: LCSH: Business enterprises--Finance. | Venture capital. |
    Angels (Investors) | Strategic planning.
Classification: LCC HG4026 .T456 2020 (print) | LCC HG4026 (ebook) | DDC 658.15/224--dc23
LC record available at https://lccn.loc.gov/2020034087
LC ebook record available at https://lccn.loc.gov/2020034088

British Library Cataloguing-in-Publication Data
A catalogue record for this book is available from the British Library.

For any available supplementary material, please visit
https://www.worldscientific.com/worldscibooks/10.1142/11874#t=suppl

Desk Editors: Aanand Jayaraman/Nicole Ong

Typeset by Stallion Press
Email: enquiries@stallionpress.com

Printed in Singapore

About the Authors

Francesca Tenca is Assistant Professor at Politecnico di Milano. She has specialized in seed and informal financing and has research and teaching experience in entrepreneurial finance and startup creation and scaling up. Francesca has been a visiting scholar at the Vlerick Business School (Belgium) and at the Imperial College of London. She is member of the Italian Association of Managerial Engineering (AiIG) and of the Academy of Management. Her primary research focus is Entrepreneurial Finance, including Business Angels, Venture Capital financing and Alternative Finance. Her particular research focus is on investors' decision-making in the crowdfunding phenomenon, its drivers of success and its linkages with "traditional" sources of entrepreneurial finance.

Vincenzo Butticè is Assistant Professor at Politecnico di Milano. His main research interest is in entrepreneurship and entrepreneurial finance. His research work has appeared in several journals, such as *Entrepreneurship Theory & Practice*, *International Small Business Journal* and *Research Policy*, among others. Vincenzo has been actively involved in a number of projects funded by the EU and other public and private institutions. Vincenzo is Vice-Director of the Observatory on Climate Finance and senior researcher of the Observatory on Drones at Politecnico di Milano. He is a member of the Italian Association of Management Engineering (AiIG), the Entrepreneurial Finance Association and the Academy of Management Association (AoM). Vincenzo teaches Energy Economics at the M.Sc. level in energy engineering at Politecnico di Milano and he is also lecturer of entrepreneurial finance at the MIP School of Management.

 **Massimo G. Colombo** is a full Professor of Entrepreneurship, Entrepreneurial Finance and Innovation Economics at Politecnico di Milano. He also is the Vice-Dean for Research & Rankings at Politecnico di Milano School of Management. His main research interests are in the organization, financing and growth of high-tech entrepreneurial ventures, strategic alliances, acquisitions and open innovation. Prof. Colombo is author (or co-author) of numerous books and articles in leading scientific journals including *Science*, the *Strategic Management Journal*, the *Strategic Entrepreneurship Journal*, *Entrepreneurship Theory & Practice*, the *Journal of Business Venturing*, the *Journal of Industrial Economics*, *Research Policy*, *Small Business Economics* and many others. He has acted as the scientific coordinator of several research projects funded by public institutions, such as the European Commission and the Italian Ministry of Education, University and Research, and private firms. Presently, he is a member of the scientific board of the Horizon 2020 RISIS project. He has provided scientific advice to prominent governmental institutions, like the European Court of Auditors, the European Investment Fund and ANVUR, the regulatory agency of Italian universities and public research organizations. He has advised the Japanese government and co-chaired the Think20 tracks on promoting small and medium enterprises' research and development and innovation programs and promoting support for startups.

Annalisa Croce is Associate Professor of Business Organization at Politecnico di Milano. Her research is concerned with several major research areas, spanning topics that include corporate and entrepreneurial finance, corporate governance and economics of innovation. She has studied these topics mainly empirically, making use of a wide range of empirical methodologies. She is co-author of more than 30 publications in international scientific journals, including the *Journal of Business Venturing, Research Policy, Entrepreneurship Theory and Practice, Journal of Corporate Finance, Small Business Economics* and *Journal of Product Innovation Management,* among others. She is Associate Editor of the *Journal of Small Business Management.* She has participated in numerous research projects, promoted by the European Commission, the Italian Ministry of Research (MIUR) and various private and public institutions. In particular, she participated in the FP7 VICO research project on "Financing entrepreneurial ventures in Europe: Impact on innovation, employment growth, and competitiveness" (Scientific coordinator: Prof. Massimo G. Colombo) and in the FP7 RISIS project on "Research infrastructure for research and innovation policy studies". She is Director of the Part-time Executive MBA at MIP, Politecnico di Milano, and a member of the Scientific Committee of the Observatory on Climate Finance.

Massimiliano Guerini has been an Assistant Professor at the Politecnico di Milano since 2015. Much of Massimiliano's research focuses on the role of entrepreneurial finance in supporting entrepreneurial activity and the performance of entrepreneurial ventures. He has studied whether and how different financing sources for startups (e.g. venture capital, angel financing and crowdfunding) contribute to the removal of innovative startups' financial constraints, as well as the implications of government initiatives for entrepreneurial activity.

He has published in the *Journal of Business Venturing, California Management Review, Journal of Corporate Finance, Research Policy* and *Small Business Economics,* among other journals. Massimiliano has participated in numerous research projects, promoted by the European Commission and various private and public institutions. He is a member of the Italian Association of Management Engineering (AiIG). He regularly teaches Industrial Economics and Entrepreneurial Finance at the MIP School of Management.

Giancarlo Giudici is Associate Professor of corporate finance at Politecnico di Milano. He belongs to the faculty of MIP Graduate School of Business where he teaches finance. He has written several articles in domestic and international journals on the topics of entrepreneurship, corporate financing, listings and initial public offerings, venture capital and crowdfunding. He is the Director of the Italian Observatories on Mini-Bond and Crowdinvesting at Politecnico di Milano School of Management. He led several projects financed by public and private entities on the topics of competitiveness and firm financing. He is Adjunct Professor at the Ton Duc Thang University in Ho Chi Minh City (Vietnam).

Contents

Chapter 1

Introduction

1.1 Why We Study Startups

New firm creation has for many years captured the interest of policy makers in different countries. The reason is that newly born companies, the so-called startups, represent a fundamental engine of economic development. We all agree that a startup is a company in its first stage of operations, but that should not be enough to define a startup. Although there is no clear and quick definition of a startup, as sales, profits and employee figures are vastly different among businesses and sectors, the core feature of startups is the focus on growth and innovation, which differentiates them from small businesses.[1]

Startups create, develop and disseminate new products, processes and technologies, generating positive effects in terms of innovation and competitiveness in the whole economic system in which they are embedded. Furthermore, they play a fundamental role in the creation of new jobs, especially high-skilled ones.

For these reasons, it is not surprising that policy makers are interested in supporting entrepreneurship, acting on those

---

[1] Robehmed, Natalie (16 December 2013). "What is a Startup?". *Forbes*. Retrieved 31 March 2020.

obstacles that prevent the creation of startups, their survival in the first difficult years of life and, of course, their growth.

Among the main difficulties that startups face, it can be argued that the lack of an adequate level of funding is one of the main problems. In the absence of an adequate supply of external finance, the survival and, above all, the growth of startups can be difficult, if not compromised.

But, what are the reasons that make it particularly difficult for startups to access external finance? The reasons are many and complex. We have tried to summarize them in the following three key concepts: uncertainty, complexity and the lack of positive cash flows.

Uncertainty refers to the fact that startups have never operated in the market, which makes it difficult for external financial providers to have realistic estimates of the expected return on their investment. Complexity applies particularly to those startups that operate in technologically advanced sectors, and refers to the difficulty that potential investors find in understanding and evaluating the commercial potential of pioneering or extremely advanced technologies. Finally, during the first years of life, it is difficult for a startup to generate stable and predictable cash flows, which makes it difficult to meet the financial obligations for debt repayment. Thus, investments in startups are characterized by a high level of risk.

Think, for example, of a startup that intends to develop and commercialize a new electro-medical device for the early diagnosis of a specific disease. In this context, it can be assumed that the time to market will be particularly long. In addition to the time necessary for technology and product development, it is also necessary that the device meets all the regulatory requirements, ensuring accurate diagnosis for the patients. The process for obtaining these authorizations generally takes years, and it is by no means taken for granted. A private investor is not necessarily willing to wait for years before obtaining uncertain (risky) financial returns on the investment, even if potentially very high. However, it would be of great interest for policy makers to favor the growth of this type of business, as there would be high benefits for society as a whole.

In summary, financial resources are a fundamental element to enable a startup to operate successfully in the market. However, startups, especially high-technology ones, typically do not have sufficient financial resources and suffer from a funding gap. Different actors in the entrepreneurial finance ecosystem help these companies to thrive, providing the funding they require to start the business and grow even further.

In this context, the objectives of entrepreneurial finance, which we can define as the process of making financial decisions that apply to startups, are twofold.

On the one hand, entrepreneurial finance studies how entrepreneurs and managers of startups can make efficient financial decisions and consciously choose the best financing channels to alleviate the funding gap. In doing so, it tackles important questions that challenge founders: how much money can and should be raised; when and by whom should it be raised; what is an acceptable valuation of the startup; and how contracts and exit decisions should be structured.

On the other hand, entrepreneurial finance takes into account the investment decisions of financial providers and institutions that are interested in investing in new, innovative and high-growth potential companies.

In essence, entrepreneurial finance is a specific but very important topic of corporate finance. In fact, the growing importance of high-technology startups as drivers of growth and economic development has generated an increasing interest in corporate finance among scholars, entrepreneurs, investors and policy makers.

1.2 Book Outline

The book is divided into five main chapters. Each of these chapters identifies a major entrepreneurial finance topic. Chapter 2 gives an overview of the entrepreneurial finance ecosystem and its main actors. Chapter 3 provides a summary of the main financial theories that can be applied to startups. Chapters 4 and 5 focus on the most important financial actors presented in Chapter 2. In particular,

Chapter 4 deals with debt finance, while Chapter 5 is about other sources of financing, analyzing in greater depth the investment process of each of its key players, i.e. venture capitalists, business angels and crowdfunding. Chapter 6 covers the topic of business incubators, organizations that help startups through different support services, instead of directly providing capital.

Overall, Chapters 2 and 3 are more theory based and aim to provide a comprehensive perspective on the entrepreneurial financial ecosystem and the background knowledge to understand the investing process of the different financial actors. In contrast, the following chapters are more practical. They include definitions, key data, examples and empirical evidence intended to provide the readers with the proper terminology as well as both basic and more sophisticated knowledge about the functioning of the different financial channels for startups.

This book assumes that readers have familiarity, but not mastery, of the basic concepts covered in undergraduate courses of finance, statistics or accounting (for example, the book assumes that the reader knows the difference between "debt" and "equity"). Key terms are given in **bold type** with, when needed, their acronym in parenthesis. All acronyms, key terms and other significant terms are listed in the glossary. Each chapter (or relevant subchapter) ends with a short summary, references and a self-assessment questionnaire to not only verify the learning of key concepts but also encourage further readers' critical thinking.

Chapter 2

The Entrepreneurial Finance Ecosystem

2.1 Introduction

Before describing the **entrepreneurial finance ecosystem**, it is important to make a premise. Although capital is the lifeblood of every firm, liquidity is especially critical for startups. A startup typically incurs a lot of expenses before and right after incorporation, while generating profits (if any) and positive cash flows only in the medium and long term. In such circumstances, the personal funds of the entrepreneur and the capital she manages to collect from relatives and friends can hardly be enough to start the business and are, in most cases, insufficient to sustain the venture's growth until profits transform into significant cash flows. Table 2.1 summarizes the typical sources of cash inflows and outflows of a business.

Profit is the surplus after all expenses are deducted from revenue and represents the economic performance of the business. Cash flow is given by the inflow and outflow of money from a business; it is necessary for daily operations, taxes, purchasing inventory, paying employees and sustaining all the other operating costs. Thus, even if profit and cash flow are related, they are not the same and there is a temporal mismatch in their generation, which makes it one of the priorities of the entrepreneur to constantly find the money to keep the business running.

Table 2.1:   Source of cash inflows and outflows.

	Cash inflows	Cash outflows
Operating	• Revenues • Decrease in inventory and receivables • Increase in payables	• Cash costs (purchases of raw materials and services, labor) • Taxes • Increase in inventory and receivables • Decrease in payables
Investing (CAPEX)	• Asset divestment (tangible, intangible, financial)	• New capital expenditures (tangible, intangible, financial)
Financing	• Raising money (equity, debt)	• Pay back funds (loan principal repayments, interests, buybacks and dividends)

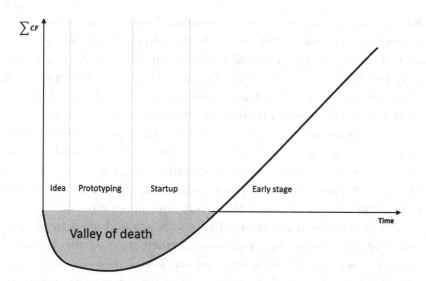

Figure 2.1:   Startup valley of death.

During the initial phases, a **startup** must operate without any existing revenue, relying on the initial invested capital. This period is commonly called **valley of death** (Figure 2.1). During this time, the startup has begun operations, but has not yet generated cash flows. Actually, the startup is burning cash to launch the business, commercialize its products and make itself recognizable to potential customers (e.g. R&D, prototyping and marketing). The cash burn rate (i.e. the monthly flow of money needed by the startup) is an essential parameter to estimate the money to be injected in the venture. Surviving the valley of death is an important achievement for a startup. It requires one to begin to generate sufficient cash to make the business self-sustainable before the money invested runs out or to raise additional funds.

Having determined that it is essential to understand and plan for the financial needs of one's business, particularly in the startup phase, the entrepreneur must carefully consider which channels are available to raise money. The choice of these financing channels in the early stages can be a key element to achieve high performance.

Figure 2.2 shows the different financial channels available for companies according to the stage of their **lifecycle** and the **amount raised**. A more complete description of these stages is found in Table 2.2.

First, startups can use the **debt capital market** or the **equity capital market**. Debt capital takes the form of bank loans and bank overdrafts or other securities, such as **minibonds**. The first form is

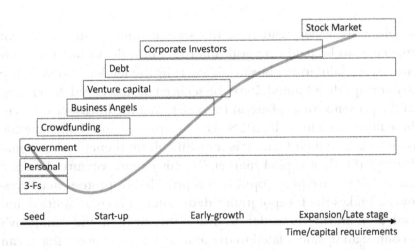

Figure 2.2: Financial sources along the company lifecycle.

Table 2.2:   Stages of growth.

Stages of growth	
Seed stage	A limited amount of capital is given to an entrepreneur as proof of concept. If the initial efforts are effective, next phases include product creation, market analysis and putting together a management team.
Startup stage	Capital is provided for developing the company. The products are usually in testing, pilot production or may be just commercialized. The company may be in the process of incorporation or may already be in business.
Early-growth stage	Capital is used to finance the initial expansion of the company. The company is producing and shipping and has growing working capital. It may or may not be showing a profit. Typically, the company has negative cash flows.
Expansion/late stage	Capital is used to finance a fairly stable growth of the company, i.e. the company is still growing, but at a slower rate than in the early-growth stage. The company may or may not be profitable, but it is likely to be more profitable than in the early-growth stage. Typically, the company has positive cash flows. It may also be considering going through an IPO.

largely more widespread than the second one. In any case, debt finance must be paid back with interest, but it does not convey any ownership claim to the business's assets by the lender, and thus, the investor upside is limited. It can be secured or unsecured depending on the presence of a **collateral** (i.e. assets that the borrower offers to the lender to secure a loan). Since startups have low if any tangible assets to secure their loans, it is very difficult for them to raise capital through the debt capital market. To this extent, **venture debt** is a viable, but not frequent, option. It is provided by professional investors and takes the form of junior debt. Interest is compounded and paid at maturity, in order to leave the cash in the company's accounts; an upside related to the venture performance is that it can be contracted, in order to reward the high risk of the loan.

Concerning the equity capital market (also known as risk capital or liable capital), a distinction can be made between **private** and **public capital markets**. In the former case, equity capital is provided by specialized intermediaries, such as venture capitalists, corporate investors or business angels. In the latter case, we refer to IPOs (initial public offerings) and, more recently, crowdfunding. In this case, external investors become the company's owners, i.e. the money invested is provided in exchange for ownership and control of the company.

Second, the different actors in the entrepreneurial finance ecosystem specialize in different stages of the development of companies (see again Figure 2.1). At birth, the so-called **seed stage**, when there is only an entrepreneurial idea not yet transformed into a company, the most typical source of financing, in addition to the personal savings of the founders, is the capital provided by family members and friends, the so-called **3Fs capital** (Family, Friends and Fools).

The first actual external investors with whom startups come into contact are typically **business angels**, who provide capital ranging from few tens of thousands of euros to a few hundred thousand euros. Business angels are competent individuals, often with previous managerial and entrepreneurial experience, with relevant personal financial resources, who invest minority shares in startups, generally in the seed or, less often, in the **startup phase**. They are a link between the 3Fs and venture capitalist investments. Business angels are increasingly organized into angel groups or angel networks. These organizations pool and invest the capital of their members, allowing economies of scale to be achieved both in the selection of investment targets and in the coaching of the invested companies.

In recent years, **crowdfunding** has also been an interesting channel for seed financing. Crowdfunding is an open call, generally through dedicated platforms on the internet, for obtaining financial resources, which can take different forms. For our purposes, the two most important types of crowdfunding are equity crowdfunding and reward-based crowdfunding. In equity crowdfunding, a percentage of the company's risk capital is offered in subscription to the crowd. In this respect, equity crowdfunding resembles a small-scale IPO. In reward-based crowdfunding, instead, startups ask the crowd for financial resources in return for the future delivery of a product or service.

Venture capitalists typically intervene at a later phase, the so-called startup phase, when the company needs more financial resources to develop its business, even if there are some venture capitalists already active in the seed phase. The amount of financing ranges from about 500,000 euros to a few million euros, generally growing from one round of financing to the following round and can reach significantly higher figures when the company has to scale up its business (e.g. to internationalize). In the **early-growth phase** and in the following **expansion/late phase,** we also saw the presence of **corporate investors** (i.e. a particular type of venture capitalist). Venture capitalists are the most important players in the entrepreneurial finance ecosystem. They are specialized professional investors, who provide risk capital to high-technology startups characterized by high potential, but also of high risk. They generally acquire minority shares in such companies, but protect their investments through appropriate clauses, such as veto rights over certain strategic decisions like acquisitions or divestments of strategic assets. The receipt of a venture capital round is a fundamental milestone in the life of a startup and leads to a drastic change in its governance and way of operating. Companies receive a considerable infusion of financial resources. Thanks to these resources, the coaching activities carried out by venture capital investors and their network of contacts, the startup can expand its operations and sustain future growth. However, venture capital is not without disadvantages. In particular, the entry of a venture capitalist into the company's capital structure leads to principal–principal agency costs, as the financial and strategic objectives of venture capital investors may differ from those of entrepreneurs. Despite these disadvantages, venture capital is considered a fundamental element in the development of high-potential, high-growth startups and, more generally, an important factor in stimulating economic growth.

Finally, startups and companies can use additional sources of finance throughout their lifecycle: bank loans and public subsidies (government). However, as mentioned earlier, bank loans are more difficult to obtain for startups and are generally of limited size, due to the difficulties that banks encounter in financing these types of companies. Banks provide two types of services to startups. On the one hand, they provide loans acting as **commercial banks**. On the other hand, startups use the services of **investment banks**. In this role, banks can help startups to issue loans in the form of bonds, such as minibonds. In addition, investment banks are a key player in exit operations. They help these companies at a later stage of their lifecycle to organize their stock market listing through the IPO or alternatively to find a buyer for an exit transaction through company acquisition by a third interested party.

Public subsidies, instead, are provided by local, national and supranational governmental institutions and they are of different types. There are automatic subsidies, such as tax credit for R&D expenses or tax advantages for startups, and selective subsidies, which are granted to high technology in return for the presentation of specific research and innovation projects. An important example of the latter category is the Horizon 2020 program managed by the European Commission.

Before looking more closely at the different actors involved in the entrepreneurial finance ecosystem, it is worth examining the conditions under which startups can completely avoid resorting to the external capital market. First, especially at birth, startups can use the founders' personal funds and the financial resources acquired through social relationships from relatives and friends (i.e. the 3Fs). In addition, startups can organize their operations in order to minimize their financial needs. These creative financing mechanisms are known as **bootstrapping**.

This concept was first used in an article of the Harvard Business Review (Bhidé, 1992). The author argued that although policy makers and entrepreneurship courses emphasize fundraising from venture capitalists and business angels, most of the traditional startups do not need such substantial capital, especially at the beginning.

Moreover, entrepreneurs who use bootstrapping require a particular way of thinking and approach to successfully implement it, while many principles used in corporate finance are not helpful in this regard. From this initial study, the knowledge on bootstrapping has evolved and various forms of bootstrapping have emerged not only with specific benefits but also with obvious limitations. In any case, financing through bootstrapping, even for a limited period of time, should not be underestimated. For example, the studies from Harrison *et al.* (2004) and Gartner *et al.* (2008) show that about 95% of US startups use bootstrapping, at some point, to finance their activities.

There are different types of bootstrapping (e.g. Winborg and Landstrom, 2001; Auken, 2005):

1. *Founder financing methods*: use of founders' personal funds and credit cards, loans from family and friends, relatives working for non-market salary, withholding founders' and managers' salary.
2. *Minimizing investments*: use of office space or machinery and equipment in collaboration with other startups, minimizing investments in inventory or employees (e.g. use of low-cost resources such as student internships in place of internal staff).
3. *Minimizing account receivables*: obtain advance payment from customers for products or services that will be supplied later on, use of specific financing methods to finance the working capital (e.g. invoice trading).
4. *Delaying payments*: delay payments to suppliers, leasing of machinery and equipment.
5. *Customer-related methods*: tapping resources from customers, receiving prepayments for prototypes.

Financing via bootstrapping has various advantages. By operating in a situation of constrained resources, companies become more efficient and creative and learn to rely on DIY. In addition, the absence of external financing, particularly of external equity capital, avoids a particular type of cost known as principal–principal agency cost, which arises because of conflicts between shareholders with different objectives. However, bootstrapping also has some clear disadvantages. First of all, it has a high opportunity cost because entrepreneurs invest their time to obtain savings that could prove to be marginal, taking it away from activities with higher added value. In addition, companies that rely on bootstrapping forgo mentorship and other benefits provided by external investors, such as venture capitalists or business angels. Low-cost or shared resources can also prove to be unproductive. Finally, the lack of resources reduces the company's flexibility and may prevent entrepreneurs from taking advantage of interesting business opportunities that may present to the company. Of course, the use of bootstrapping also depends on the entrepreneurial ecosystem in which the startup is embedded; it is used more or less in different countries, in relation to the economic and industrial system, startups' growth orientation and future perspective, and the availability of alternative financial sources, such as a viable crowdfunding market.

We can therefore conclude that bootstrapping is not an efficient solution if a startup needs non-marginal financial resources. In this case, startups are forced to resort to the external financial market.

2.2 Summary

- During the initial phases, a startup must operate without any existing revenue, relying on the initial collected capital. This period is commonly known as the "valley of death". During this time, the startup has begun operations, but has not yet generated cash flows, burning the initial money raised.
- Startups can resort to the external capital market to finance their operations and investments. There are two main markets: the debt capital market (bank loans and bonds) and the equity capital market (capital provided by specialized financial intermediaries, who buy shares of the company).
- Moreover, startups and companies use different financial channels according to the stage of their lifecycle and the investment amount needed. The most important players are as follows: in

the seed stage, the so-called 3Fs, business angels and crowdfunding; in the startup phase, venture capitalists and business angels; in more late stages of their life, corporate investors, banks and the public market (IPO and the stock market). Throughout the lifecycle, companies can use bank loans (with some limitations for startups) and public subsidies.

- Startups can also avoid resorting to the external capital market by performing bootstrapping. It consists of different methodologies aimed at organizing companies' operations in order to minimize their financial needs. These include using founders' capital, minimizing investments and account receivables, delaying payments and implementing customer-related strategies.
- Besides various advantages, bootstrapping is not an efficient solution if a startup needs non-marginal financial resources.

Self-assessment Questionnaire

2.1 Why is there a temporal mismatch between companies' profits and cash flow generation and what are the consequences for startups?

2.2 What does it imply for startups and their founders to resort to the debt capital market or to the equity capital market? Can all typologies of startups leverage each capital market indifferently?

2.3 According to the different phases of the company's lifecycle, what are the optimal financial channels to collect external funds for startups and companies?

2.4 *True, false or uncertain:* Venture capitalists are fundamental equity financial providers, which is most valuable in the startup stage of a company's lifecycle.

2.5 *True, false or uncertain:* The use of bootstrapping must be cautiously evaluated by the entrepreneur on the basis of her background and network, the local financial ecosystem, the industry and specific business activity.

References

Auken, H. V. (2005). Differences in the usage of bootstrap financing among technology-based versus nontechnology-based firms. *Journal of Small Business Management, 43*(1), 93–103.

Bhidé, A. (1992). Bootstrap Finance: The art of startups. *Harvard Business Review, 70*(6), 109–117.

Gartner, W. B., Frid, C. J., & Alexander, J. C. (2008). Financing the emerging business through monitored and unmonitored sources of funding. *Frontiers of Entrepreneurship Research, 28*(1), 4.

Harrison, R. T., Mason, C. M., & Girling, P. (2004). Financial bootstrapping and venture development in the software industry. *Entrepreneurship & Regional Development, 16*(4), 307–333.

Winborg, J., & Landström, H. (2001). Financial bootstrapping in small businesses: Examining small business managers' resource acquisition behaviors. *Journal of Business Venturing, 16*(3), 235–254.

Chapter 3

Theoretical Background

3.1 Introduction

In this chapter, we provide an overview of the main financial theories and models that explain the demand and supply of capital with a particular focus on the entrepreneurial finance ecosystem. These theories (the pecking order theory, the signaling theory and the agency theory), in fact, can be valid for incumbent firms, but are particularly useful to understand the investing process of the different financial actors in the startup ecosystem. We begin the chapter with the key concept of information asymmetries, which deeply affect the capability of startups to access financial sources.

Startups, particularly high-technology ones, are characterized by information opacity, which makes it difficult for them to access external sources of finance. This results in a capital market imperfection, where capital providers fail to provide startups with the money they need. The resulting financial constraints suffered by startups prevent their growth. Of course, this funding gap is especially problematic at the founding stage and in the early years of a company's life.

We say that there are **information asymmetries** between entrepreneurs and capital providers when information is unevenly shared between the two subjects and this lack of information prevents the capital providers from financing companies. Information asymmetry may refer to a high degree of uncertainty related to the business's technology, the market and/or the entrepreneurial/ management team. In the first period of a company's life, information asymmetries are more marked, also due to the reluctance of entrepreneurs, who are better informed about their business, to disclose specific technological knowledge and development plans that risk their exposure to competition. For these reasons, the main source of capital for companies at foundation, in addition to the personal funds of entrepreneurs themselves, is the money provided by their relatives and friends.

However, not all startups necessarily experience the same level of uncertainty. Uncertainty and information asymmetries are expected to be high in companies characterized by innovative products or innovative business models, companies characterized by a broad knowledge base and intangible assets (e.g. intellectual property), which are especially more difficult to evaluate, and companies operating in sectors characterized by a long time to market (e.g. pharmaceutical, energy industries). Information asymmetries make it extremely difficult for these companies to obtain sufficient bank loans. That is the reason why these types of startups in particular finance themselves through risk capital obtained from business angels and venture capitalists, who are willing, for a "piece" of property in the company and, therefore, the promise of future high enough returns, to provide risky investments.

Finally, it is worth pointing out that information asymmetries are not unidirectional, but in many situations capital providers have larger knowledge of the market in which the startup is going to enter. Business angels and venture capitalists, for example, may have great experience from the past in running a business or insights into market trends and potential customers' preferences from similar investments.

In the following paragraphs, we present different theoretical frameworks that explain why and how entrepreneurs seek capital and how they may overcome information asymmetries.

3.2 The Signaling Theory

To understand **signaling theory**, let us start with an example. Consider a market in which companies of different quality operate. For the sake of simplicity, suppose that half of the companies active in the market have good-quality projects characterized, for example, by a low probability of failure and/or high returns. The remaining half of the companies have low-quality projects with a high probability of failure and/or low returns. Investors know that only half of the companies operating in the market are of high quality, but they are not able to distinguish between high-quality and low-quality companies. Consequently, they indiscriminately demand a premium in terms of additional returns on the financial resources provided to companies to cover the risk of investing in a low-quality company. Low-quality companies find this premium reasonable and are willing to accept the financing. This is not the case for high-quality companies, as the premium paid to obtain the financial resources is not proportional to the quality of their innovative projects. As a result, high-quality companies prefer to withdraw from the market. In this way, they leave the field to low-quality companies, which will be financed at a high price congruent with the low quality of their innovative projects.

In a situation of information asymmetry such as that described, what can high-quality companies do to obtain financial resources at prices proportional to the high quality of their innovative projects?

The signaling theory, originally developed by the Nobel Prize winner Michael Spence (1973), provides an interesting answer to this question.

High-quality companies can report their quality by making investments that are inefficient for low-quality companies. In other words, companies can buy a quality signal.

For low-quality companies, obtaining such a signal is very expensive, while it is much cheaper for high-quality companies to obtain it. For such companies, acquiring the signal is profitable, while it is not profitable for low-quality companies. Consequently, at the market equilibrium, only high-quality companies acquire the signal, making their high quality clear to potential investors.

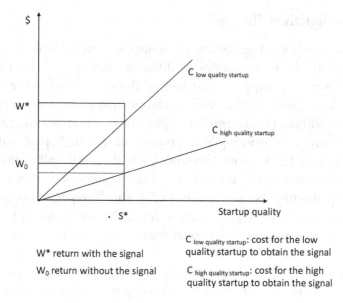

W^* return with the signal

W_0 return without the signal

C low quality startup: cost for the low quality startup to obtain the signal

C high quality startup: cost for the high quality startup to obtain the signal

Figure 3.1:   Value and costs of signals.

This situation is described in Figure 3.1. In the figure, W_0 shows the amount of returns for a startup in the absence of signals. If the startup is able to report its high quality by acquiring the signal S^*, it will be able to reduce its financing costs by increasing its returns from W_0 to W^*. Thus, the value of the signal is given by the difference between W^* and W_0. The purchase of the signal S^* is profitable only for high-quality startups, as the $C_{\text{high quality startup}}$, the quality cost of the signal, is lower than its value. On the contrary, for low-quality startups, buying the signal is not profitable, as its cost $C_{\text{low quality startup}}$ is excessive, i.e. higher than its value.

Collateral is a typical signal in the case of bank loans. It provides the bank with insurance, typically a physical asset, which the bank can acquire at a higher priority than other equity investors in the event of bankruptcy of the startup. Only high-quality startups have an interest in providing the collateral, thus indicating their quality. However, high-technology startups rarely have physical assets that can be used as collateral, as most of their investments are intangible or firm-specific and, therefore, have low liquidation value. However, the entrepreneurial finance literature has highlighted a number of ways in which high-technology startups can signal the quality of their projects (e.g. Connelly *et al.*, 2011). The most important signals include the following: obtaining a patent or a public grant through a competitive bidding process, winning a startup competition, becoming affiliated with a prestigious entity, such as a university, or forming an alliance with a prestigious partner. Under certain conditions, the human capital of the company's founders or board members can also be considered a quality signal to attract external investors.

3.3 The Pecking Order Theory

The **pecking order theory** (or financing hierarchy) was developed independently by Myers and Majluf (1984) and Fazzari and colleagues (1988) in the 1980s, and offers an interesting synthesis tool to analyze the equilibrium between the supply and the demand of capital by entrepreneurial ventures. The theory is based on the idea that information asymmetries create a gap between the cost of internal capital, provided to the company by entrepreneurs and their relatives and friends, and the cost of external capital, whether it is debt capital provided by banks or equity capital provided by business angels and venture capitalists. This different cost of capital creates a hierarchy of sources of finance: the preferred source of finance for high-technology startups is the internal capital, as it is the cheapest source. This is followed by the debt capital and then by the equity capital.

The financing hierarchy, and the market equilibrium behind it, is illustrated in Figure 3.2.

The figure shows on the X axis the quantity of capital necessary to finance the activities of the startup and on the Y axis the cost of capital. Startups may have a low capital demand indicated by line D_I or a high capital demand indicated by line D_{II}.

The marginal cost of internal capital is indicated by C_I. It does not vary with the increase in the capital invested by the entrepreneurs in the company and is equal to the opportunity cost of this

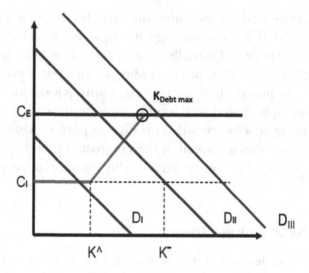

Figure 3.2: Pecking order framework.

capital, i.e. the return obtained in its best alternative use. If the startup has a demand for capital represented by line D_I, it will finance its activities exclusively through internal capital, which, as mentioned above, is the lowest cost source of capital. In fact, the amount of capital needed to finance the company's activities is less than the amount of internal capital available $K^\wedge$. In other words, in this case, the internal capital is sufficient to efficiently finance the startup's activities.

If, on the contrary, the startup's demand for capital is represented by the line D_{II}, the startup cannot finance its activities solely from internal capital. To do so, it would be necessary to have a quantity of internal capital K'' that exceeds the maximum quantity of internal capital available, equal to precisely $K^\wedge$. In this case, in equilibrium, in addition to the internal capital, the startup uses bank debt. Contrary to what happens for the internal capital, the supply curve of bank debt is positively inclined. In fact, banks are willing to offer more capital to the startup only at a growing marginal cost, because of the information asymmetries existing between entrepreneurs and the banks themselves. Moreover, banks are not willing to lend beyond a certain amount. If the amount of internal capital available was sufficient to finance the startup's activities, the company would use the amount of capital equal to K''. However, as stated above, this amount is not available. Consequently, in equilibrium, the startup will use a smaller amount of capital, and will seek and obtain a debt amount that covers the needs of capital not covered by the internal capital.

Finally, let us consider what would happen if the startup wanted to further scale up its activities and, thus, increase the demand for capital, demanding the amount of capital D_{III}. In this case, not only the internal capital but also the bank debt would be insufficient to finance the startup's activities (the maximum amount of debt financed by the bank lies at the intersection between the line C_E and the positively inclined line representing the cost of debt capital). The startup would therefore be forced to use external equity capital provided by venture capitalists and business angels at the cost C_E. External equity capital is the most expensive form of financing for a high-technology startup, for two reasons. First, the information asymmetries described above imply a lemon premium that reduces the company's pre-money valuation. In other words, business angels and venture capitalists will be willing to invest in the startup, but with the financial resources they make available, they will require a high percentage of its risk capital, leading to a large dilution of the share held by entrepreneurs. Second, to protect themselves against the business risk of failure and the behavior of entrepreneurs that may not be in line with their objectives, they will require a number of control rights. These rights constrain the freedom of action of entrepreneurs, thereby reducing their personal well-being. The advantage over other forms of financing is that the provision of equity capital by business angels and venture capitalists can be considered substantially infinitely flexible. In other words, at the cost C_E, these investors are able to meet all the financing needs of the company.

The evidence provided by Robb and Robinson (2014) on the financing of small American companies, innovative or not, is in line with the predictions of the pecking order theory. The capital provided by entrepreneurs and other insiders is 47% of the total financial sources used, by far the largest source of financing for entrepreneurs, followed by trade credit with 22%. Bank loans have a share of only 17%. Business angels are present in about 6% of companies, while venture capitalists are present in less than 1%.

However, other empirical studies conducted in different countries led to contradictory results; the theory, in fact, was first developed for large and mature firms. Small high-technology startups are subject to different market dynamics, and over time, the studies have led to a change in their opportunities, choices and costs of external capital (Mason, 2017). As a consequence, some modified versions of the pecking order theory have emerged.

Howorth (2001) finds that, in small firms, the pecking order works in a truncated way. Because of the reluctance of entrepreneurs to give up control over their company due to the entrance of external equity investors, we see a truncation at the point of debt capital.

Paul *et al.* (2007) show that startups are constrained in their choices of external financing, leading to a bridged pecking order, where firms, after running out of internal funds, avoid debt and use only equity finance. This is because small high-technology startups in particular find it more difficult to obtain credit from banks (having high-risk projects, high information asymmetries and little collateral to offer as guarantee) than equity capital from specialized investors (e.g. venture capitalists or business angels), who are also able to add value to the company with their business experience and networks. Moreover, debt represents a liability on the company's assets and entrepreneurs may prefer to place a self-determined limit on that.

Additionally, new forms of equity financing available to high-technology startups, such as equity crowdfunding (see Section 5.7 of Chapter 5), have exacerbated this mechanism. Companies may avoid financing at the early stage with debt and use, instead, a "bundling" of external sources of equity capital, such as crowdfunding, financing from syndicates and networks of business angels, who are able to contribute larger amounts of funds than single-business angels, and early-stage venture capitalists (Mason, 2017).

Finally, Carpenter and Petersen (2002) have advanced that an inverse pecking order framework is likely to happen for startups. The preference for entrepreneurs is reversed in favor of equity before debt and internal funds. In fact, external equity providers have the advantage to bring more than just financial resources to the table; they have superior knowledge about the market, on how to manage a business and a wide network of contacts to support startups' development compared to banks, who are just passive capital providers.

3.4 The Agency Theory

The **agency theory** (Jensen and Meckling, 1976) explains that there is a principal–agent problem when a person or an entity, the agent, makes decisions, in the name and on behalf of another person or entity, the principal. The agent will make decisions that are in line with her personal interests, but may not be in line with the objectives of the principal. If the decisions taken by the agent differ from those optimal for the principal, the principal will bear a cost, known as the agency cost. Again, the source of agency costs is an information asymmetry that makes it difficult for the principal to effectively monitor the agent's behavior and prevent him/her from making decisions that diverge from those optimal for the principal himself.

Agency costs exist if, first, the agent is motivated to act in her own personal interest instead of making decisions in line with the principal's objectives; second, the agent's objectives differ from those of the principal; third, the principal fails to observe the agent's behavior, but only observes the results of her decisions; and finally, if there is no perfect information on what determines the agent's decision results. In these circumstances, any divergence between the results obtained by the agent and the results expected by the principal cannot be immediately traced back to divergences between the decisions taken by the agent and those optimal for the principal. In order to realign the interests of the agent with her own interests, the principal may design incentive contracts, which link the agent's remuneration to the results of her decisions. The fact that the results of the agent's decisions are subject to uncertainty makes such contracts costly for the principal. Thus, the remuneration expected from the agent must be sufficient to ensure that she bears the burden of that uncertainty.

In the field of entrepreneurial finance, there are two typical examples of principal–agent relations. First, venture capitalists manage the financial resources provided by other financial intermediaries (that we call "investors" here), such as banks, insurance companies, family offices or sovereign wealth funds. In this relationship, the latter are the principals and have the objective of maximizing the returns on their investment, while the managers of the venture capital funds are the agents. They could manage these financial resources by pursuing personal objectives and consequently making investment decisions that differ from those optimal for their investors. Contracts governing the relationship between the managers of venture capital funds and their investors are designed in such a way as to induce the managers to maximize the returns on the financial resources invested through appropriate incentives. The most typical incentive that investment managers have is the carried interest. It is typically equal to 20% of the difference between the proceeds obtained from the exit from the investments made and the capital provided to the venture capital fund by its investors. Carried interest is the main component of the remuneration of VCs and creates a powerful incentive to maximize returns on investment through successful exits.

A second important agency relationship in the entrepreneurial finance landscape is between the managers of venture capital funds and the entrepreneurs, who own the companies that are the target of venture capitalists' investments. In this case, we can talk about a principal–principal agency relationship, since both entrepreneurs and venture capitalists are shareholders of the same company. In this situation, why should the interests of the two main shareholders differ? To answer this question, it should be remembered that the life of a VC fund is typically 10 years. At the end of the fund's life, the fund is liquidated, and the financial resources are distributed to those who have invested in the fund after the payment of carried interest to the fund's managers. Consequently, VCs are not permanent investors. They acquire shareholdings in young, innovative companies in order to rapidly grow their valuations and achieve a successful exit. As a result, the objectives of VCs may differ from those of entrepreneurs if they are interested in a more gradual and delayed growth. In addition, the dilution of the equity share of entrepreneurs as a result of VC investments could reduce the incentives for entrepreneurs to devote all their time, attention and energy to developing their portfolio companies. Also, in this case, the design of appropriate contractual clauses allows one to reduce agency costs by realigning the objectives of entrepreneurs and VCs. Perhaps the most typical example of such clauses is staging. In fact, VCs usually do not finance companies by investing in a single solution, but dilute their investment in a series of rounds. Investments subsequent to the first round are made generally at a valuation (i.e. the equity value of the company before the additional capital is transferred to the company) higher than the initial one, but only if the entrepreneurs are able to reach contractually defined milestones, such as the creation of a functional prototype or the achievement of a predefined sales target.

3.5 Summary

- High-technology startups are characterized by information opacity, which makes it difficult for them to access external sources of finance.
- Information asymmetries emerge between the entrepreneurs and the capital providers when information is unevenly shared between the two subjects. This lack of information prevents the capital providers from financing high-technology startups.
- Information asymmetry may be related to a high degree of uncertainty in the business's technology, the market and/or the entrepreneurial/management team.
- Information asymmetries are more marked in the early period of a company's life, in startups characterized by innovative products and business models, in startups and companies

characterized by a broad knowledge base and for specific sectors (e.g. pharmaceutical, energy industries).

- Information asymmetries may also be bidirectional, such as in many situations capital providers have more knowledge than the entrepreneurs, for instance, about the market in which they operate.

- In this chapter, we reviewed three theoretical frameworks, the signaling theory, the pecking order theory and the agency theory, which explain why and how entrepreneurs seek financial resources and may alleviate information asymmetries.

Self-assessment Questionnaire

3.1 Why do information asymmetries emerge between entrepreneurs and investors and why are they especially significant for startups?

3.2 What are the characteristics that an effective signal must have according to the signaling theory? Is the entrepreneur's level of education an effective signal for investors such as VCs? What about the receipt of a seed round of financing?

3.3 Why are the traditional pecking order theory principles questioned in today's entrepreneurial finance landscape?

3.4 In the relationship between entrepreneurs and VCs, there are high principal–principal agency costs. What can entrepreneurs and VCs do to lower these costs?

References

Carpenter, R. E., & Petersen, B. C. (2002). Is the growth of small firms constrained by internal finance? *Review of Economics and Statistics, 84*(2), 298–309.

Connelly, B. L., Certo, S. T., Ireland, R. D., & Reutzel, C. R. (2011). Signaling theory: A review and assessment. *Journal of Management, 37*(1), 39–67.

Fazzari, S., Hubbard, R. G., & Petersen, B. (1988). Investment, financing decisions, and tax policy. *The American Economic Review, 78*(2), 200–205.

Howorth, C. A. (2001). Small firms' demand for finance: A research note. *International Small Business Journal, 19*(4), 78–86.

Jensen, M. C., & Meckling, W. H. (1976). Agency costs and the theory of the firm. *Journal of Financial Economics, 3*(4), 305–360.

Mason, C. (2017). *Financing the Scale-up of Entrepreneurial Businesses: Beyond the Funding Escalator,* CEEDR/ISBE seminar on SME Finance 10 Years After the Financial Crisis, Middlesex University, 20 June 2017.

Myers, S. C., & Majluf, N. S. (1984). Corporate financing and investment decisions when firms have information that investors do not have. *Journal of Financial Economics, 13*(2), 187–221.

Paul, S., Whittam, G., & Wyper, J. (2007). The pecking order hypothesis: Does it apply to start-up firms? *Journal of Small Business and Enterprise Development, 14*(1), 8–21.

Robb, A. M., & Robinson, D. T. (2014). The capital structure decisions of new firms. *The Review of Financial Studies, 27*(1), 153–179.

Spence, M. (1973). Job market signaling. *Quarterly Journal of Economics, 87,* 355–374.

Chapter 4

Debt Financing

4.1 Introduction

Debt is an instrument widely used by companies of all sizes. For example, Vanacker and Manigart (2010) analyze the financing events of about 2,000 high-growth Belgian companies and show that nearly half of these events are related to the growth of debt financing. However, many entrepreneurs claim they are unable to acquire the necessary funding from banks, even if they are willing to pay a steep interest rate on loans. This phenomenon is known as **credit rationing**: banks simply limit the amount of loans to businesses. This practice clearly discourages the birth of new companies and limits their growth once they are born. As a result, national governments and supranational institutions, such as the European Commission, have implemented support measures, such as loan guarantees to small and medium-sized firms, with the aim to make banks less reluctant to provide these loans.

Before examining credit rationing in depth, it is important to understand its origin. The relationship between banks and startups is characterized by significant information asymmetries that generate both adverse selection and moral hazard problems.

Adverse selection problems arise due to the presence of an information asymmetry between entrepreneurs and banks. The entrepreneur clearly has inside information on the quality of her business, the risks of her innovative projects, her skills and capabilities, and the commitment she intends to put into the growth of her venture. Banks, on the contrary, do not have all these pieces of information and, therefore, are unable to make a precise assessment about the quality of the loan applications they receive. It should also be considered that entrepreneurs, who apply for a loan, have incentives to exaggerate their skills and their commitment in order to obtain the loan. Furthermore, they are not willing to disclose to the banks sensitive and confidential information about the potential of their innovative projects, as they fear that any leakage of such information would increase the risk that third parties would appropriate their technological knowledge. It should also be considered that young and small companies have no credit assessments. Such assessments are provided by agencies like Moody's or Standard & Poor's, but they evaluate the credit of only large incumbent companies due to their large debit exposure. Finally, in a competitive market, no single bank has the incentive to invest in collecting information about the reliability of an entrepreneur who requests a loan, as it would expose itself to the risk of free riding by other banks.

Moral hazard problems in the relationship between entrepreneurs and banks can be illustrated by the following situation. If an entrepreneur is able to obtain a loan from a bank, he must pay the interest on the loan received at a fixed time (e.g. quarterly) and must then return the capital to the bank at the end of the loan. In summary, in exchange for the loan received, the entrepreneur must pay the bank a sum equal to D, inclusive of interest. In the most common case, the company created by the entrepreneur has limited liability. Thus, in the event of bankruptcy, the banks cannot retaliate on the entrepreneur's personal wealth, but can only make demands on the liquidation value of the company's assets. Suppose that the entrepreneur invests the sum received from the bank in an innovative project. If the yield on the project is less than D, the company becomes bankrupt, all assets and properties are liquidated and the bank collects the liquidation value of the assets, which is usually much lower than the original value of the loan plus interests accumulated, D. If instead the project is successful, the entrepreneur gets a remuneration equal to the difference between the value of the project V and D. Consequently, after obtaining a loan, an entrepreneur could be induced to select riskier projects, which not only have a higher value, V, in favorable conditions but also have a higher probability of default. In fact, unlike the bank, the entrepreneur fully benefits from the high returns of such projects in favorable conditions, while the limited liability places a lower limit on the losses that the entrepreneur would incur in unfavorable conditions.

> **Credit rationing** is a state of equilibrium, generated by the fully rational optimal response of banks to the existence of information asymmetries, in which banks limit the amount of loans to borrowers.

4.2 Credit Rationing

In this paragraph, we discuss the different types of credit rationing (Stiglitz and Weiss, 1981) enforced by banks and their effects on the financing of high technology.

There are two main types of credit rationing. The first is when, at a certain interest rate set by the bank, companies request a loan of a certain amount, but they obtain a smaller loan (Jaffee and Russell, 1976). The second is when some of the companies requesting a loan do not receive it, although they appear to be completely identical to those that have obtained the loan and are willing to accept a higher interest rate (Stiglitz and Weiss, 1981).

The two types of credit rationing are described in Figure 4.1.

Figure 4.1 shows the demand for loans by companies and the supply of credit by banks. In the absence of information asymmetries, the market equilibrium is identified by the intersection between the demand and the supply curves. The companies will obtain loans in amounts equal to Lm at the price Dm. Dm represents the amount that entrepreneurs undertake to give back to the banks at the expiry of the loans, including the interest paid on the loans obtained.

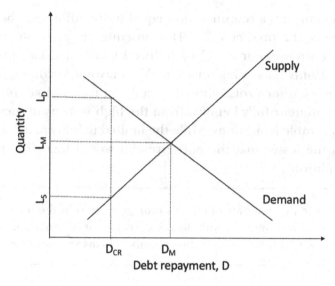

Figure 4.1:   Supply and demand for loans.

In the presence of **type 1 credit rationing**, the banks will offer each entrepreneur a loan of an amount equal to LS at the Dcr price. At this price, each entrepreneur expresses a loan request higher than Lm and equal to LD. The difference between LD and LS measures the extent of credit rationing introduced by banks.

In the presence of **type 2 credit rationing**, LS represents the number of companies that in equilibrium obtain a loan from banks at the Dcr price. At this price, the number of companies requesting a loan is higher and equal to LD. Also, in this case, the extent of the credit rationing is measured as the difference between LD and LS.

Let us now consider how the presence of information asymmetry leads to credit rationing. We focus initially on type 1 credit rationing. Suppose that the expected returns of a startup, but also the risks associated with the probability of bankruptcy, increase with the size of the loan requested from the banks. Suppose also that there are two states of nature: a favorable state and an unfavorable state. In the favorable state, the entrepreneur will get a return R, which is greater than the amount D he must return to the bank in exchange for the loan received. This return increases with the loan amount.

In the unfavorable state, the company goes bankrupt and cannot repay the loan received, i.e. D is equal to 0. Once a loan is obtained from the bank, the entrepreneur can choose more or less risky investment projects. If the entrepreneur is protected by limited liability, he will be more interested than the bank in returns that occur in favorable states of nature and less interested in losses that occur in unfavorable states. We define as "optimal" the loan amount that maximizes the sum of returns for the entrepreneur and the bank. The entrepreneur has an incentive to ask the bank for a loan of a greater amount than the optimal one, as it allows him to obtain higher returns in a favorable condition, in spite of higher bankruptcy risks. This situation would penalize the bank. As a result, the bank uses credit rationing and limits the amount of the loan itself, in order to contain the risk that the company will go bankrupt and the loan will not be repaid.

We consider now type 2 credit rationing. We make the following assumptions. Entrepreneurs are risk neutral and ask the banks for a loan of an amount L to create a new business. Every entrepreneur has a single project. All projects have the same expected returns. However, some projects are riskier than others, as some entrepreneurs have less skills and experience to carry out their projects. These entrepreneurs also have a lower opportunity cost to pursue an entrepreneurial career, given the salary they can get in the labor market. This situation is described in Figure 4.2.

The PE curve shows the expected return for an individual as a function of individual abilities x when he chooses a career as a hired worker. It, therefore, represents the opportunity cost of being an entrepreneur. The EN curve shows how the expected return of each individual changes when he chooses an entrepreneurial career. Individuals with abilities lower than x-tilde will prefer the entrepreneurial career, as the expected returns in this profession are higher than the relative opportunity costs. Entrepreneurs know their abilities perfectly and therefore the risk profile of their projects, while the banks do not have this information. What the banks know is simply the distribution of individual abilities in the population of entrepreneurs who apply for a loan. What happens when banks

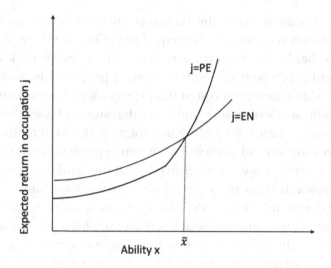

Figure 4.2:   Cause of type 2 credit rationing.

decide to increase the cost of loans? The expected returns associated with the entrepreneurial profession are reduced for all entrepreneurs. However, the individuals who suffer the most from this increase are those with the best skills, for which the entrepreneurial choice has the highest opportunity cost. For a certain number of such individuals, the expected returns associated with the entrepreneurial career are reduced below the relative opportunity cost, causing them to give up the creation of their company. However, such individuals would have been the best customers for banks, pursuing less risky projects. The result is that the set of projects released by entrepreneurs is characterized by a higher degree of risk, which leads to a reduction in the expected returns on the loans granted by banks. Accordingly, banks have no incentive to increase the cost of loans beyond the level that maximizes their profits, which can lead to a situation of type 2 credit rationing.

4.3 Debt Instruments for Startups

So far, we have understood that debt financing is difficult to obtain for startups and may not be appropriate for certain startups. For example, the earlier the stage of the company and the lower/less tangible the collateral, the more expensive the terms of the debt will be, or debt may not be a viable option at all. Nevertheless, there are some kinds of startups, e.g. companies with consistent cash flows or operating in certain sectors, that might use debt financing. Moreover, there are some debt-based forms, aside from bank loans, which may be specifically suitable for startups. We briefly discuss these debt instruments in the following paragraphs.

First, certain startups may use bank debt. Bank loans fall into two types: secured business loans and unsecured business loans. The former are guaranteed against an asset, such as the entrepreneur's house or assets belonging to her company. Depending on the type and value of assets the entrepreneur can put up as security, even substantial amounts of debt can be borrowed. However, these types of loans have clear disadvantages. Since secured business loans are often granted only if the entrepreneur commits a personal guarantee on the loan, they may lead to catastrophic consequences for the entrepreneur in case of default. Unsecured business loans, instead, are not guaranteed against a specific asset, so they may be characterized by a comparatively higher interest rate and a more limited loan amount. In fact, the amount and the interest rate will depend on the entrepreneur's personal credit rating and the startup's creditworthiness. In either case, banks typically have long lists of requirements that a startup must fulfill, before accepting the loan, along with a lengthy application procedure.

A second option suitable for startups is invoice financing (or invoice trading). In this case, a third party, i.e. a financial intermediary, buys the outstanding invoices and lends money to the startup against their value with an interest. Invoice financing is best suited to B2B companies that sell on credit and have a good selection of reputable customers. However, there are a broad range of providers in the market that are also willing to work with startups. This form of debt is useful to finance working capital with quick access to financial resources (even within 24 hours) and no requirement of providing any assets as collateral. Thus, particularly in sectors in which companies may take a long time to get payments from their customers, invoice trading can support the startup's cash flows in the short term. There is, of course, a cost, as the startup does not collect the full income on its sales, but the financial intermediary will take a cut for monthly interest rate and service fees. Recently, online platforms, similar to crowdfunding ones, have developed to provide invoice trading to startups. However, given the low familiarity and appeal of account receivables to the retail investors and the prospect of generating big profits at a relatively low risk, this market is dominated by institutional investors.

Another source of debt for startups that has recently expanded enormously is peer-to-peer business lending (P2P). P2P is a form of lending crowdfunding (see Chapter 5.6), where a P2P lending platform links creditworthy businesses that are searching for a loan to individuals who want to invest. Lenders can gain higher interest rates, while startups can repay funds at lower interest rates, compared to the ones offered by banks. The interest rate on loans depends on the creditworthiness and performance of the company. The main advantages are a fast process to obtain the loan, a lot faster than obtaining a bank loan (usually a couple of weeks, once the application has been approved), and the possibility to adapt the loan terms, such as specifying the duration of the repayment period and/or no early repayment costs. However, there are also disadvantages. If the company is unable to repay the loan, the entrepreneur becomes directly responsible to reimburse the loan with her personal assets (in case of unsecured loans) or with the company's assets (in case of secured loans). Moreover, any late or missing repayments would be reported in the entrepreneur's credit scoring, making it more difficult to obtain another loan in the future.

Finally, the last option available for startups and, in general, small and medium-sized companies is the minibond. Minibonds are bonds, i.e. medium-/long-term debt securities issued by unlisted companies for development plans, extraordinary investment activities or refinancing operations. Minibonds allow startups to open up to the capital market. Their issue has advantages for businesses in terms of debt diversification, reduction of dependence on banking and other debt sources and tax incentives, such as the deductibility of interest expenses and issue costs. However, a startup that wants to issue a minibond must become more transparent, making its past and future financial and business plans available to potential investors. For this purpose, the company is typically supported by a financial advisor, who carries out an analysis on the feasibility of the minibond issue and helps the company prepare the business plan. Investors, in this case, are typically institutional investors and high-net-worth individuals.

4.4 Summary

- Many entrepreneurs are unable to acquire the necessary funding from banks, even if they are willing to pay a steep interest rate on loans.
- Credit rationing is a state of equilibrium, generated by a rational response of banks to the existence of information asymmetries, in which they limit the amount of loans to companies.
- These information asymmetries are the results of both adverse selection and moral hazard problems. The former is generated because the entrepreneur has more information on the quality of her company than the bank, while the latter are caused by the fact that an entrepreneur, after obtaining the debt, could be induced to select riskier projects, which have a higher return in favorable conditions, but a higher probability of default in an unfavorable state. While the bank may lose the whole credit in case of default, the limited liability places a lower limit on the losses that the entrepreneur would incur.
- Type 1 credit rationing occurs when, at the interest rate set by the bank, companies request a loan of a certain amount, but obtain a smaller loan.
- Type 2 credit rationing occurs when some of the companies requesting a loan do not receive it, although they appear to be exactly identical to those that obtain the loan and are willing to accept higher interest rates.

- Among the debt instruments available to startups, we acknowledge, in addition to bank loans, invoice financing (also called invoice trading), P2P business lending and minibonds.

Self-assessment Questionnaire

4.1 Describe the reasons why banks perform credit rationing.

4.2 *True, false or uncertain:* The 2007 US subprime mortgage crisis is an example of an unforeseen moral hazard. As property values plummeted (when the housing bubble burst), borrowers ended up indebted deeper on their loans. Homes were worth less than the amount owed on the underlying mortgages. Thus, many house owners saw this as an incentive to walk away from their loans, as their financial burden would be limited.

4.3 *True, false or uncertain:* In the presence of type 1 credit rationing, the entrepreneur has an incentive to ask for a greater loan than the optimal level, because she can always find high-value projects.

4.4 *True, false or uncertain:* Type 2 credit rationing happens when banks, which cannot distinguish entrepreneurs' abilities, increase the cost of loans up to the point that the "best" individuals decide not to purse entrepreneurial projects.

References

Jaffee, D., & Russell, T. (1976). Imperfect information and credit rationing. *Quarterly Journal of Economics, 90,* 651–666.

Stiglitz, J. E., & Weiss, A. (1981). Credit rationing in markets with imperfect information. *The American Economic Review, 71*(3), 393–410.

Vanacker, T. R., & Manigart, S. (2010). Pecking order and debt capacity considerations for high-growth companies seeking financing. *Small Business Economics, 35*(1), 53–69.

Chapter 5

Equity Financing

5.1 Introduction

In this chapter, we analyze in depth the characteristics and investment process of the different actors of the entrepreneurial ecosystem that finance startups with equity capital. Sections 5.2–5.5 are devoted to venture capitalists. To this actor, we dedicate a longer discussion to analyze the phases of the investment process, the different typologies of VCs and their impact on invested companies. Section 5.6 deals with business angels and finally Section 5.7 analyzes crowdfunding.

5.2 Venture Capital

Venture capitalists are a fundamental player in the entrepreneurial finance ecosystem. Venture capital has been defined by Mason (2006, p. 357) as follows:

> **Venture capital:** Finance that is provided on a medium- and long-term basis in exchange for an equity stake in a venture, to finance the venture's startup or early-growth phase, in high-technology and high-growth-potential sectors.

Unlike other actors in the entrepreneurial finance landscape, such as business angels, venture capitalists are full-time professional

41

investors, who raise capital from different investors and financial institutions, such as insurance companies, banks, pension funds, corporations and high-net-worth individuals, and invest it in entrepreneurial ventures with the aim of obtaining a financial return. They make their profits from exiting their investments, by selling their stake to public markets or to another buyer (e.g. another company), when the company's share price at exit is higher than when the shares were acquired.

Although venture capitalists differ from one to another, they have some common characteristics:

- VCs invest through equity capital; debt capital can also be used in the investments, but usually for a minority part.
- VCs hold a minority stake, while the entrepreneur continues to have control over her venture.
- VCs invest in high-technology, high-risk sectors and in companies with a potential to achieve relatively rapid growth.
- VCs are active partners; they usually sit on the board of directors, and they monitor and add value to their portfolio companies though their knowledge, experience and rich network of contacts.

Venture capitalists differ across many dimensions. These dimensions include the amount of funds under management (i.e. the capital raised from their investors), the investment experience, the size of the cross-border investment activity, the reputation deriving from the success of previous investments obtained through billionaire IPOs or acquisitions with high valuation of the acquired company, and their governance.

With regard to the governance, we distinguish **independent VCs** from **captive VCs**, for which the VC fund is under the control of an external organization. In addition, this last category can be further split according to the type of the control organization, such as corporate, bank-affiliated and governmental venture capitalists. In summary, four types of venture capitalists are present in the market:

1. **Independent venture capitalists (IVCs)**, such as Sequoia, Kleiner Perkins, Accel partners or Sofinnova. These independent venture capitalists are the most widespread type of VCs within both the US and the European entrepreneurial finance ecosystem.

2. **Corporate venture capitalists (CVCs)**, such as Google Ventures or Intel Capital. These types of VCs are subsidiaries or business units affiliated to a large industrial enterprise.

3. **Bank-affiliated venture capitalists (BVCs)** are similar, but the controlling enterprise in this case is a financial institution, such as a bank or an insurance company. An example is UniCredit evo (equity venture opportunities) founded by the UniCredit Group, a major Italian commercial bank, in 2016 to invest in FinTech startups.

4. **Governmental venture capitalists (GVCs)** are VC funds controlled by public institutions. They can be a national government, as the Finnish SITRA, or a local government, such as Finlombarda (a GVC controlled by the Italian Lombardy region).

These four VC types differ significantly from each other depending on the objectives and impact of their investment activity. These differences are summarized in Table 5.1 with reference to the intensity of the financial objectives, the type of strategic objectives and the ability of investors to mobilize new resources and expertise in favor of their investees.

IVCs pursue the objective of maximizing the financial returns from their investment activity through successful exits, whether they result in an IPO or in the acquisition of the invested company. Capital gains realized in this way not only allow the IVC to be remunerated but they also signal to third parties the VC's ability to make successful investments and thus help to attract new financial resources to create investment funds. From this point of view, newly founded VCs, not having an established reputation, can have the strategic objective of showing their quality to potential institutional investors through a successful rapid exit, a phenomenon known as

Table 5.1: Typologies of venture capital.

	IVC	CVC	BVC	GVC
Strategic objectives	Raising additional capital from institutional investors, fast exit	Access investees' advanced technology	Generate demand for bank services	Social and political objectives
Relevance of financial objectives	High	Low	Low	Low
Resources and capabilities	Capabilities and business contacts of the IVC investor	Resources, capabilities, business contacts of the parent company	Resources, capabilities, business contacts of the parent bank	Capabilities and business contacts of the GVC investor

"grandstanding". Grandstanding orientation can easily collide with the entrepreneurs' objective to grow their business more progressively, generating significant principal–principal agency costs. The main added value that IVCs offer to their portfolio companies is through coaching. Their value is useful in areas where entrepreneurs do not have specific skills such as strategy, management and finance. In addition, IVCs provide social capital that can be used in the invested firm to expand resources and skills.

For all captive VC investors, the intensity of financial objectives is generally lower than the intensity of strategic objectives. The fundamental objective pursued by CVCs is to open a technological window to the research and development activities carried out by the invested company. From this point of view, the CVC is an important element of open innovation strategies of large multinational technology companies. Indeed, they are able to provide invested companies with complementary resources for the innovation activities they carry out. For example, they can manage relations with regulatory authorities, produce the products developed by high technology in which they have invested and distribute those products on a global scale. A potential threat for the companies that are invested by a CVC is the possibility of the investor using its technological skills to absorb the innovative knowledge developed by the invested company and exploiting it autonomously. This phenomenon, known as "swimming with the sharks" syndrome, presents significant risks for the invested company, especially when the investor is a competitor, even if only in potential.

Also for BVCs, VCs affiliated with banks or other financial institutions, the strategic objectives are generally more important than the financial ones. In this case, the fundamental objective is to generate a demand for the financial services traditionally offered by the parent company, typically in commercial banking or investment banking activities.

Finally, GVCs typically pursue social or political objectives, such as the creation of new jobs or the economic development of the territory in which they are established, be it a region or a nation.

5.2.1 *The venture capital market*

Venture capital funds are now the main source of financing for startups, with a total investment in 2018 of $160 billion, according to recent estimates by KPMG.

Globally, the venture capital market has followed the trend of the economic cycle. Historically, the maximum market expansion was at the beginning of the 2000s and the period immediately preceding the bursting of the internet financial bubble. With the bursting of the bubble, there was a collapse in both the number of investments and the amounts invested by VCs, from which the market recovered only in the following 10 years. Since the second half of the 2000s, taking into account the net of the normal seasonality of the market and a downturn during the 2008 financial crisis, the venture capital market has grown steadily in terms of capital invested.

However, it is interesting to note that the number of investments has declined considerably since 2015. This trend is partly explained by an increase in the capital invested in each round of financing. In part, it is also due to the growing VCs' propensity to invest in late-stage startups, which are typically less risky, but at the same time require larger investments. A third reason for the increase in the average investment size is the change of VCs' investment focus. VCs have invested more and more in the software and biotech industries, and less in startups in the consumer goods and commercial services sectors. The former are, in fact, sectors with higher average financial needs. This increase in the average investment size has been observed both in the US and in the European market.

The venture capital market is also known to be a geographically concentrated market. In the US, venture capital investments are especially concentrated in three metropolitan areas: San Francisco, Boston and New York. Startups located in these regions typically have higher success rates and are therefore more attractive to investors. Startups located in these three areas alone receive about two-thirds of all venture capital investments on US territory. Since 2015, this share has even increased due to some large investments in startups located in this area, such as Uber and Dropbox.

Historically, VCs have been much less active in Europe than in the US market, with Europe characterized by a total volume of investments that is about one-third of the North American market. Even within Europe, there is a strong geographical concentration.

The most developed venture capital market in Europe is the United Kingdom, which alone represents more than 50% of the continental market in terms of both the number of investments and the capital invested. Other important hubs in Europe are the French and German ones.

The geographical concentration is also found within individual countries. The UK market is largely concentrated in the London area, and in France and Germany, the main financing VC hubs are Paris and Berlin, respectively.

Over the years, there has also been an increase in the valuation of startups invested by VCs. This trend, which has been confirmed in all rounds of financing, has been particularly pronounced in the case of investments in late-stage financing rounds, i.e. in all those cases where startups had already received several rounds of previous funding. The increase in startup valuations is in part associated with the change of focus by VCs that in recent years have invested in industrial sectors, where the expected exit values are higher (such as artificial intelligence and automotive), and is in part attributable to the tendency to invest repeatedly in startups called **"unicorns"**. These are companies with a pre-money valuation (i.e. the company value before the venture capital infusion of funds) of more than one billion euros. Clearly, the investment in these startups influences the valuation statistics. There has been a proliferation of such start-ups over the years, from a couple of new unicorns a year to several dozen from 2015 onward. About 50% of these new unicorns operate in the software sector, but there are also examples in other indus-tries, such as the production of consumer goods and the energy sector.

Moreover, the increased investments of VCs during all financing rounds have led to a reduction in the average age of startups that become unicorns, and, at the same time, a reduction in the number of average rounds before a startup becomes a unicorn.

5.2.2 *Creation of the venture capital fund*

In the venture capital cycle, the initial fundraising phase is funda-mental to allow the VC management team (also referred to as VC managers) to collect the necessary financial resources both for future investments in startups and to cover the costs of managing the fund, which are not negligible. The creation of a new VC fund is generally promoted by professionals who had a career in finance, in business banks or consultancy firms, or in the venture capital industry itself. Therefore, they have developed the skills and a net-work of contacts that can be useful for building a new fund. VC management teams tend to be quite small, because if too many people were involved it would be difficult to maintain the fund's cost structure without eroding the fund's profitability. Administrative, legal and other compliance services are performed either outside or by the staff of the group, if the fund is promoted by a structured organization. In general, the VC fund managers can also co-invest in the fund itself, with a minority stake, and this is a positive signal appreciated by investors, because it helps to align the incentives with the managers.

As stated earlier, VC funds can also be promoted by banking groups, with the aim of diversifying their activities, by industrial groups, with the aim of creating opportunities for technological innovation and synergies with their business, or by public entities, such as supranational, national or regional bodies, with the aim of stimulating innovation and entrepreneurship and, in general, the economy. In all these cases, the most relevant part of the fund's financial resources will be made available by the promoters themselves.

The typical structure of a VC fund consists of two levels. The first level is made up by the VC managers, who are in charge of the operational management of the fund, and, in particular, of the search for investment opportunities, the selection of the investments and the management of the investments afterward. The second level is made up by the investors, who provide most of the capital of the fund. The governance of this structure can be articulated in different forms. In Figure 5.1, we see a typical VC fund structure.

More specifically, a vehicle is set up to be the **general partner (GP)** of the fund (also called the VC firm): it is the company where the managers and fund promoters are represented. The vehicle can also co-invest in the fund, for a minority stake. The GP holds the control of decisions (investments, exits, etc.) and the administrative liability on the fund.

Investors, on the contrary, become **limited partners (LPs)**: they supply most of the fund's financial resources, but delegate the fund's operations to the managers. However, this does not mean that LPs do not have any right to control what happens. To reduce the risk of opportunistic behavior by the VC management team, they are represented in an investment committee that has the right to express an opinion, more or less binding, on the proposed investments and other decisions. Under certain conditions, LPs are also

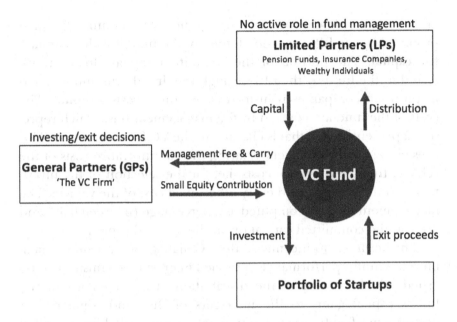

No active role in fund management

Limited Partners (LPs)
Pension Funds, Insurance Companies,
Wealthy Individuals

Capital | Distribution

Investing/exit decisions

General Partners (GPs)
'The VC Firm'

Management Fee & Carry

VC Fund

Small Equity Contribution

Investment | Exit proceeds

Portfolio of Startups

Figure 5.1: Venture capital fund structure (adapted from Da Rin *et al.*, 2013).

able to vote to change the VC management team, in the event of serious disagreements.

The vehicle can be set up either in the home country of the VC managers or abroad, depending on the fund's investment choices (e.g. the fund may concentrate investment operations on the domestic or the international market) and on tax considerations related to the taxation regime on capital gains. The fund must then be organized in compliance with the legislation in force in the chosen jurisdiction. For instance, the fund can be set up as an asset management company, authorized and supervised by the country's financial market regulator, or in a more flexible way, but with less guarantees for the investors, such as a holding company, for instance, with two classes of shares and with a particular statute to replicate the dual structure of the fund.

When a fund is first raised, the LPs promise to provide a certain amount of capital, which will be provided either on a set schedule or at the discretion of the GP. These periodic capital provisions are known as **drawdowns**, or takedowns. The total amount of capital promised by the LPs over the lifetime of the fund is called **committed capital**. The portion of the committed capital already transferred to the fund by the LPs through the drawdowns and invested in portfolio companies is instead called the **invested capital**. The costs of the fund are covered by the **management fees**, which represent a percentage fee that is charged to the VC fund every year. This is used to pay the managers' salaries, the administrative costs of the vehicle, the due diligence costs, i.e. for the selection of the investments in the startups, and every other fixed cost of the vehicle. The management fees are computed as a percentage (between 0.5% and 2%) on the committed capital or on the invested capital.

Furthermore, to incentivize the VC management team to maximize the fund's performance, a **carried interest** mechanism is established, which consists of the distribution of a percentage of the fund's capital gains to the managers of the fund, similar to a performance fee. In practice, a percentage rate is established, called **hurdle rate** (normally between 6% and 8%), which is applied and compounded annually to the amount initially invested. The fund's final proceeds, up to this amount, are distributed entirely to the LPs of the fund. The exit proceeds that eventually exceed this amount, and this will clearly happen when the fund performs very well, are distributed among the LPs (usually 80%) and the VC managers (usually 20%) as a reward for having generated a yield above the hurdle rate.

Of course, there is no guarantee to obtain such returns, and therefore the actual performance of the fund will be determined by the successes, or failures, of each investment.

5.2.3 *The fundraising phase*

In the fundraising phase, the management team of the VC fund, once the entrepreneurial project has been defined, is engaged in the search for possible investors.

Sophisticated investors represent the typical target. On the one hand, they have adequate financial resources to invest in the fund and, on the other hand, they are well aware of the risk that investing in high technology entails. Examples of typical investors are banking foundations, family offices (i.e. managers of wealthy families' assets), insurance companies, pension funds, funds of funds (funds which in turn invest in other funds) and high-net-worth individuals (i.e. individuals who can count on relevant personal assets or substantial income). The main objective for these investors is to diversify their asset portfolio. Financing venture capital is usually not their main purpose, but they want to reduce the overall risk of their portfolio and diversify the investments into unrelated activities and they are willing to allocate some money even to risky investments. However, having no time or skills to do it directly, they prefer to invest in a fund, together with other subjects.

There are also public bodies that, with the policy objective of favoring investment in venture capital, invest resources in dedicated funds. An example, at the European level, is the European Investment Fund. However, the commitment from public entities is generally limited to the 50% of the size of the fund and the VC team must, therefore, demonstrate that it is also capable of gathering resources in the market of private investors.

To convince potential investors to invest in the fund, there are two effective strategies. First, it is important to demonstrate the quality of the project, which is described in a document, the **investment memorandum**. This is a sort of "prospectus" that is presented to a very small circle of potential investors. It contains the objectives of the fund, the startup selection strategies (in which sectors, in which phases of the lifecycle), how to help invested companies create value, what kind of financial instruments will be used (equity, convertible debt, warrants, etc.), the curricula of the VC managers, the fund cost structure and governance mechanisms.

The second instrument to attract investors is to show the VC management team's previous track record. If the managers of the fund have previously managed other funds, demonstrating fundraising skills, selecting winning projects and obtaining exits with high capital gains for investors, it becomes much easier to raise a new fund. The fundraising is, instead, more difficult for "first-time teams" that cannot show previous investment experience.

In the first phase of the fundraising, a series of **soft commitments** is collected. These are expressions of interest, not yet contractually binding, declared by potential investors. A very important role in this initial phase is played by the **anchor investors**, who are the first subscribers of the fund, who act as catalysts for other possible investors. Their presence is a positive signal, especially if they are prestigious investors. When the VC team has reached a sufficient number of investment commitments, the first closing of the fund can take place. It means that, from this moment, the subsequent subscriptions are binding and the operations of the fund can begin.

After the first closing, according to what is written in the investment memorandum, it is possible to make other subsequent closings, as new commitments are collected, until the fundraising is definitively closed. Starting from this moment, the only activity for the VC management team is to invest the capital collected, selecting the most promising investment opportunities.

The committed capital, as mentioned earlier, is rarely immediately paid by the investors. Most of the time, they will be asked to provide the capital only when the liquidity is needed, depending on the agreements with the entrepreneurs of the selected startups and the needs of the fund. This is useful to prevent investors from bearing an opportunity cost of capital, because if the fund immediately raises all the money, a large fraction of cash will remain unused for a certain period of time.

The size of a venture capital fund cannot be too high, nor can it be too low. Having too much money available is a problem, especially for a VC fund, because it requires the identification and selection of a large number of investments, which are difficult to manage simultaneously. On the contrary, a very small VC fund will be penalized by high fixed costs that affect its structure and harm the fund's performance for investors.

Finally, it is important to highlight that a VC fund has a definite lifetime, usually about 10 years. In the first period, the investments are selected and finalized; in the second period, the startups are supported in their growth process; in the third period, the exits take place, with the sale of the investments; and at the closing of the fund, the realized exit proceeds are distributed to the investors and the VC management team. The managers, however, have a certain flexibility in the timing of this entire process. Depending on the economic and financial cycle, which may be more or less favorable, they can accelerate or slow down the lifecycle of the fund.

5.2.4 The investment process

The VC investment process is complex and articulated. A potential target startup for a VC goes through several stages before any final decision and transfer of funds are made. These stages include the pre-screening, the formal screening, the due diligence, the negotiation of the term sheet and the final closing.

Table 5.2 provides an example of the number of investment proposals that proceed through each stage of the process for a typical VC. We consider an initial number of 1,000 proposals received per year. Of course, this first number has a wide range of variation depending on the size and reputation of the VC firm, and may vary from 100 to 1,000 or even more. In any case, the odds of reaching the second stage, the formal screening stage, are usually not higher than 10%. Of those 100 screened potential investments, about 20 will go through to the more intensive due diligence phase. Most VCs report that around another half of those 20 will reach the term sheet, which is a preliminary contract that will be further negotiated with the entrepreneur. At this point, the odds of reaching the final closing are pretty good as 9 out of 10 potential investments result in

Table 5.2:   Typical VC deal flow.

Pre-screening	1,000
Screening	100
Due diligence	20
Term sheet	10
Closing	9

a successful negotiation. Anyway, the overall chances of reaching the final closing of the investment are extremely low, below 1%.

Each subsequent stage takes progressively more work and the exact process for each stage varies considerably across VC firms.

While for a small VC firm, the process may be less structured and all partners may be involved in all stages and in the final investment decision, for the larger VC firms, this is simply not feasible. In this case, a team of junior partners, who do not take the lead on investments, have the role to screen potential investments, perform due diligence and draft the contract. Decisions at various stages (e.g. decision on which proposals pass the screening after a preliminary assessment by junior partners) then are usually made by a committee of senior partners.

In the following paragraphs, we briefly describe each stage of the VC investment process.

5.2.4.1 *Deal origination and pre-screening*

The managers of a VC fund have to seek good opportunities to invest in. The number and the quality of the proposals received, which are called **deal flow**, are therefore key elements of VC performance. In general, the better the reputation of the VC firm, the better the deal flow and the less effort the VC needs to put into finding a lot of good deals.

The main sources of deal origination include the following:

- Business plans submitted by entrepreneurs through the VC website;
- Incubators;
- Universities and R&D centers;
- Startup competitions;
- Bank advisors and other professional service providers (e.g. consultants, lawyers and accountants);
- Direct referrals from highly valuable personal contacts.

The origination is a crucial phase, since the VC management team wants to collect as many projects as possible, in order to maximize the probability of finding home runs, but the time to evaluate them has a high opportunity cost.

The investment opportunities received then go through a preliminary assessment, called pre-screening, with the aim to efficiently dismiss unrealistic, unfeasible ones, those characterized by low growth prospects and others that are out of scope of the VC firm's investment strategy (e.g. projects at the seed stage for a VC that invests in the early- or late-growth stages).

5.2.4.2 *Screening*

In the screening stage, VCs are highly selective. Only a small percentage of the proposals collected up to this point makes through the screening phase. At screening, investments are usually evaluated using the **business plan** prepared by the entrepreneur. The business plan contains an overview of all relevant facts and information concerning the business. It offers a comprehensive description of the product/service offered, future strategic plans of the company, the market in which the company operates, the background of the management team and the business financial projections. While financial forecasts are often provided, the specifics of such estimates differ greatly. For example, for later-stage businesses, forecasts may include detailed financial statements, while, for early-stage companies, the predictions are simpler and, foremost, highly sensitive to the assumptions made by the company's management team. The VC, therefore, uses not only its skills and past experience to evaluate the proposals but also a sort of "sixth sense" to recognize future "winners". Indeed, this stage requires a mix of art and science to identify potential successful investments.

Almost all VCs consider two fundamental aspects of a business opportunity:

1. The market potential, i.e. the market should be large and characterized by a growing trend.
2. The quality and track record of the startup's management team, i.e. the entrepreneurial team has enough competence and experience to execute the business plan.

In the evaluation of the management team, VCs also pay attention such that team members have complementary competence and all key company functions are covered.

These two major aspects are complemented by the analysis of other elements: customers, including the attractiveness and the likelihood of customer adoption of the new technology or product, the customer channels, the market competition and company's competitive advantages, the company's partners and their reputation, and the money available (i.e. the capital provided by the entrepreneur or other seed investors). Moreover, VCs make a preliminary assessment of the terms of the agreement, such as the presence of synergies with other VC portfolio investments, a favorable valuation of the company, the possibility to apply contractual provisions that limit the investment risk and future exit opportunities.

During the screening phase, interviews with the entrepreneur and the management team are common to clarify the managerial and technical issues contained in the business plan. The so-called "pitch" or "elevator pitch" (i.e. a brief presentation intended to showcase the company's products, technology, strategy and team to the potential investors) is the perfect opportunity to see the quality of the management team. Additionally, if necessary, more data can also be released by the entrepreneur upon the signing of a nondisclosure agreement (NDA), while the VC may be assisted by consultants and experts in the target company's technology.

A "memorandum of understanding" (MoU) is the document that may be signed at this stage. Any binding commitment for investment is released only after the complete due diligence.

The screening is one of the most time-consuming phases of the VC investment process, so VC firms (especially large VC funds) usually employ junior specialists to perform much of this task, while senior VC partners concentrate on later stages of the investment process and on the monitoring of portfolio investments.

5.2.4.3 *Due diligence*

Once VC managers have completed the initial screening successfully, the investment proposals proceed to a more detailed level of assessment. The formal due diligence aims to reduce information asymmetry between the entrepreneur and the VC, as well as the investment risk.

This phase actually requires different typologies of due diligence:

- **Business due diligence:** Study of the business model, in order to understand if the company management team's estimates about revenues and costs are affordable.
- **Technical due diligence:** Required if the technology proposed is rather specific and/or innovative.
- **Legal due diligence:** To avoid future legal troubles and assess litigation risks (e.g. patent infringement, national laws and existence of pending procedures).
- **Tax due diligence.**
- **Environmental due diligence or others:** Depending on the target company's sector.

Due diligence costs are generally paid by the VC fund managers with the management fees.

5.2.4.4 *Term sheet*

The term sheet is a preliminary contract offered by the VC to the entrepreneur. The term sheet is the most important document to negotiate with investors, as almost all of the contractual issues that matter are covered in the term sheet. It is typically non-binding, except for certain provisions, such as confidentiality and no shop/exclusivity clauses (i.e. the firm must not engage with other investors during the negotiation phase).

The document is structured in different sections, with each section providing a summary for a longer legal document that will be implemented at the closure of the deal.

The most important parts of the term sheet are as follows:

- **The offering terms:** The list of investors, the amount invested by each of them and the number of shares they receive for this amount; the company's price per share; the valuation of the company (see Section 5.2 for more details); and the company's capital structure before and after the closing (i.e. capitalization table).

- **Charter (or Certificate of Incorporation):** Establishes, among others, the rights, preferences, privileges and restrictions attached to each class and series (A, B, C, etc.) of the company's shares (e.g. liquidation preference, dividends, voting rights and other VC protective provisions).

- **Investor rights agreement:** A technical section describing a long series of rights pertaining to the VC, other preexisting investors and the founders. These rights concern, for example, the management of the company (e.g. composition/approval mechanisms of the board of directors), or what investors/founders can/cannot do in the occurrence of certain events (e.g. sale of shares by founders, sale of the company and exit).

Some VC contracts also require that VC financing will be provided to the company through a **staging** process. In this way, VC funds are provided in subsequent tranches upon the reaching of certain milestones (e.g. the development of a patent or a prototype, the development of the product to a marketable stage, the acquisition of the first major customer and the reaching of some specific level of sales). This, in turn, reduces the risks for VCs, which can wait (hold an "option" to invest) and provide the financing when more information is available and only if the thresholds set are reached.

5.2.5 *The exit phase*

The exit is fundamental for the efficient functioning of the venture capital market, since it represents the moment in which the investor succeeds in capitalizing on the financial return of its investment. The relevance of this phase is proved by the fact that the exit is already being explored and planned for in the investment phase. In fact, an investor would never decide to buy the shares of a startup without a reasonable perspective of an exit.

Usually, the exit phase takes place 4–5 years after the investment, but this period is variable, especially depending on the market momentum. In particular, favorable market conditions such as high market multiples, low volatility and an expansive economic cycle can lead to a fast exit. On the contrary, turbulence in the financial markets and a negative trend in the stock market usually push the investor to delay the exit, waiting for a more favorable time.

The choice of the timing of the exit may also generate conflicts of interest between entrepreneurs, who intend to preserve control of the company, and investors, who could force them to exit at the first favorable moment.

The exit can take place through three different alternatives. The first is the **IPO (Initial Public Offering)**, which is the listing of the company on the stock exchange market. Through a public offer aimed at the admission to the stock market, the investor can sell the shares to the public of the IPO subscribers.

The IPO is the most complex, risky and expensive alternative, because the outcome is uncertain (sometimes public offers fail due to low demand from the market), and above all the company needs to comply with the laws in various countries that regulate offers to the public by small investors, for example, usually requiring the publication of a prospectus.

The listing on the stock exchange is a "forced" step after the public offer because small investors need to hold liquid securities that can be easily sold in the future.

In the offer, technically, newly issued securities can be subscribed and therefore the company will also be able to collect new capital. Alternatively, already existing securities can be sold, such as those made available by the VC, without collecting new capital for the company. Or, both mechanisms can be used; in this last case, securities sold in the offering are partly already existing and partly newly issued.

Venture capitalists, in the case of an IPO, rarely completely exit from the investment. A portion of the shares is normally retained even after the listing. This serves to give a positive signal to the market about future expectations. A further positive signal is provided by **lock-up clauses**. These are commitments made by existing shareholders (i.e. VCs, the founders and other investors) before the IPO to not sell additional shares in the following months (usually from 6 up to 12 months), thus reducing a possible oversupply of shares in the market, which would push down their price.

The company undergoing the IPO is supported in this process by legal and financial advisors, who will take care of every phase, from the publication of the prospectus to the definition of the offer price (i.e. the price at which the shares will be traded at the opening of the exchanges the day of the listing), to the placement of securities and the final listing.

The second exit option is the **trade sale**. In this situation, negotiations open for selling the equity stake held by the VC.

Typically, potential buyers are as follows:

1. Other financial investors (e.g. funds specialized in investing in mature companies).
2. Industrial groups interested in taking control of the company, as they expect synergies with their businesses.
3. The founders themselves, who, with the support of financial intermediaries, are interested in regaining total control of the company.
4. The company management, which is called a management buyout.

Negotiations can be opened directly by the VC investors or with the help of consultants acting on a "sell-side" mandate. These consultants will contact potential buyers, looking primarily among investors with available liquidity and potentially interested in the company because of business affinity or synergies.

At the sale, VCs can take advantage of any **drag-along** and **tag-along clauses** that have been granted at the time of the initial investment. Such options allow VCs to, respectively, drag into the sale the entrepreneurs or tag along with any sales made by them. This makes it easier to negotiate and maximize the exit proceeds, as buyers typically aim to take control of 100% of the company's shares.

Moreover, it is not uncommon for investors to keep several exit options open until the last moment, i.e. negotiating with potential buyers for a trade sale, while simultaneously filing for the listing process on the stock exchange. This allows maximum flexibility and increases the bargaining power toward the potential counterparties. This strategy is called **dual track**.

A last possible exit is the failure of the investment, which happens when the startup is not able to achieve the financial objectives set by the investors. In this case, unless the original contractual terms are rediscussed, investors will cease to financially support the startup, which will ultimately lead to its default. VCs will **write-off** the investment, losing all the money invested or at least a substantial part.

5.2.6 *The exit phase: A focus on IPOs*

In this paragraph, we focus on one of the possible exit options for VC investments, the IPO.

The IPO consists of the listing of the company on a stock exchange market. Even if the IPO is not the most common exit for VC investment, it is certainly the most interesting alternative, due to its complexity and high investment returns.

A stock exchange is a centralized market where financial securities are traded. Technically, the difference between a listed company and an unlisted one is quite simple: the shares of the former company can be traded easily, quickly and at low costs, while the shares of the latter are illiquid, so trading them is complex and expensive. In reality, this simple difference involves a deep transformation for the company, with fundamental changes in the organizational structure.

The following are among the financial advantages of listing on the stock exchange: the access to an additional important financing channel, namely, the stock market, a lower cost of capital thanks to the lower risk perceived by potential investors and a greater bargaining power toward banks. The fact that the shares are listed also allows the acquisition of other companies in exchange for the company's shares, with the obvious advantage of avoiding a cash outflow.

In addition, there are also operational advantages. The IPO is a marketing event. It allows one to raise awareness about the company and its products, providing a certification of its quality. Furthermore, listed companies are able to attract more qualified managers and employees, due to the greater prestige they offer and the opportunity to assign stock options that can be easily evaluated (being equity capital listed) and liquidated.

The listing, however, bears high costs. Some costs are directly related to the listing, such as the fees that have to be paid to the stock exchange for the quotation, while some costs are indirectly related to the listing, such as the costs for the auditing of the company's financial statements once the company has listed or the costs associated with the creation of an investor relations business unit. Indeed, the legal requirements for a listed company can be very demanding, in terms of transparency and compliance (rules on investor protection, disclosure, governance and relations with supervisory authorities). For this reason, alongside the regulated exchange markets according to the European MiFID legislation, there are also unregulated markets, characterized by less expensive and less tight requirements. We can also find markets designed specifically for SMEs, and therefore particularly interesting for startups.

The listing process for a company, as shown in Figure 5.2, can be divided into a sequence of phases.

Initially, the company has to select the financial advisors that will support the company in the IPO process. Typically, these are private banks or specialized financial boutiques, in the case of small businesses. Their task is to support the company to fulfill all the requirements and compliance to list on the stock exchange as well as in the

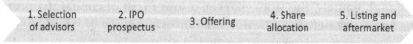

| 1. Selection of advisors | 2. IPO prospectus | 3. Offering | 4. Share allocation | 5. Listing and aftermarket |

Figure 5.2:   Phases of the listing process.

placement of the securities. It can also be convenient to hire legal or tax advisors.

The second phase is the publication of the **IPO prospectus**, which must be previously approved by the stock exchange authorities. It is a document that contains vast and detailed information with respect to the risks of the investment, the business, the ownership structure of the company, the financial statements and the conditions of the offer.

The next step is the public offering, which is usually carried out both with retail investors (small investors) and with institutional investors, such as banks and investment funds. In the case of unregulated markets, the offer may be only open to institutions.

Once the offer has been closed, it is possible to proceed with the allocation of the securities, depending on the demand collected in the previous phase. If the demand exceeds the offer, it is necessary to proceed with a rationing of the shares.

Determining the offer price in an IPO is not trivial. We are, in fact, considering a company that is not yet listed on the market; it is not known by investors and there is no reference price for the shares. Proposing a "very high" price could cause the offer to fail, with a series of sunk costs and image damages. Proposing a "very low" price would be a disadvantage for existing shareholders, including entrepreneurs and VCs, because of a dilution effect on their company stake. In order to set a fair price, an analysis of the prospective cash flows that the company will generate in the future is generally conducted. In practice, a first very important indication is given by the analysis of the **comparable multiples** (see Section 5.2 on startup valuation), i.e. the valuation multiples of similar companies, in the same sector, already listed.

It is a common practice in IPOs to initially propose an indicative price range with a minimum and maximum value in the prospectus, and set the final subscription price after the offer itself.

The IPO process finally ends with the listing phase, in the aftermarket.

A phenomenon that is often observed is the initial underpricing. At the end of the first day of listing, we observe that the market price of the IPO shares is usually larger than the offer price. This happens on average twice out of three IPOs. The finance literature explains the phenomenon of the IPO underpricing through various possible theories, which relate to information asymmetries, rationing, signaling, or models of behavioral finance and market irrationality. Another quite common effect observed in IPOs is the so-called long-run underperformance, which is the negative differential yield of newly listed companies' shares compared to the market return. This phenomenon is explained by emphasizing the greater risk that characterizes newly listed companies compared to those already listed, rather than by possible opportunistic behavior of entrepreneurs, who decide to list their companies when they see low growth opportunities in the future.

5.2.7 Summary

- VCs are professional investors, who invest in young, high-technology companies that have a capacity for rapid growth. VCs are a type of financial intermediary that performs three main functions: screening of potential investments and deciding on which companies to invest in, monitoring these companies and providing value-added services, and exiting their investments by selling the company's stake to public markets or to another buyer.
- To manage the VC fund, a vehicle is set up to be the GP of the fund (i.e. the VC firm). The GPs hold the control of decisions (investments, exits, etc.) and the administrative liability of the fund. The LPs are sophisticated and institutional investors, who commit their capital to the fund, while they delegate the management to the GPs.
- VC fund managers are compensated through the management fees and the carried interest. Management fees are usually about 2% of the fund capital. The carried interest represents the remuneration of VC managers through the capital gains made on the investments. It is most commonly set at 20% of the whole fund's exit proceeds. This compensation structure is designed to help align the incentives of VC managers and LPs.

- The VC investment process is complex and articulated and the probability for a startup to obtain the investment is very low, especially if the VC has a good reputation. The firm goes through several stages: pre-screening, more in depth screening, due diligence, negotiation of the term sheet and the final closing.

Self-assessment Questionnaire

5.1 Describe the standard structure of a VC fund. Why is it organized into a two-level structure?

5.2 Why do GPs contribute a small portion of capital of the VC fund?

5.3 Consider a VC fund with a committed capital of 100 million euros. Assuming the usual cost structure of 2% management fees and 20% carried interest, if the fund at the end of its life has realized 500 million euros in profits, how much is the remuneration for the GPs and LPs of the fund?

5.4 How does the previous answer change considering a hurdle rate of 8%?

5.5 Describe the different phases of the VC investment process. Why is it particularly difficult for startups to reach the final closing of the deal?

5.6 What are the most valuable alternative exits for VCs? What are their advantages and disadvantages?

5.3 The Impact of Venture Capital

In this section, we analyze the performance of companies that have received venture capital funding.

Generally, VC-backed companies show better economic performance than those that have not received venture capital. However, we must ask the reason why this happens. Is the better performance of companies that received venture capital due to the added value that VCs bring to those companies? Or, thanks to their screening capabilities, are VCs able to select companies that have better business opportunities and therefore perform better in the future? In other words, do VCs create winning companies, and therefore is it a matter of "treatment", or are VCs simply able to identify the right companies and focus their financial resources on them, and is it just a matter of "selection" capabilities?

Answering those questions is complicated. Two methods can be used to do this, independently or in combination. The first methodology is known as matching. For each VC-backed firm, a twin firm is identified that is similar to the company considered. The similarity with the company that has not received VC is based on a number of observable characteristics such as size, age and geographical location. This second firm is useful to simulate what would be the behavior of the firm receiving venture capital if it did not receive it. The comparison over time of the economic performance of these two companies helps to discern the effect on performance that is attributable exclusively to obtaining venture capital. The use of matching makes it possible to control the effect on the performance of VC-backed firms that is generated by observable factors. However, it may be the case that unobservable or more difficult to observe and quantify factors, such as high-quality top management teams with extensive social relations, could lead to a company having high economic performance and, at the same time, a high capacity to attract venture capital. This would lead to a spurious correlation between obtaining venture capital and the economic performance of the VC-backed company. To eliminate this second effect, an instrumental variable estimator, the second methodology, can be used. This involves identifying a variable that is positively correlated with the probability that the firm in question will obtain venture capital, but is not correlated with the economic performance of the firm itself. Exogenous shocks in the supply or demand of venture capital are the instrumental variables most often used for this purpose.

We now analyze the scientific evidence on the relationship between venture capital funding and the economic performance of companies, which have been investigated using the two methodologies described.

A study by Puri and Zarutskie that appeared in 2012 in the *Journal of Finance* provides interesting evidence on the survival and growth of US companies that obtain venture capital, using the matching methodology. In the 5 years following the acquisition of venture capital, the invested companies have higher survival rates than the twin firms without the acquired investment. They also have a fivefold higher probability of being acquired. Five years after obtaining venture capital, companies invested by venture capital are much larger than their not invested twins. Their size is more than double, measured by both employees and sales.

In a study published by the *Review of Financial Studies* in 2011, Chemmanur and colleagues analyzed the impact of venture capital on total factor productivity, the most typical indicator of business efficiency. In this case, the authors use an estimate with instrumental variables to take into account possible effects due to unobservable factors. The results of their estimates show that VCs in the US are more likely to support highly efficient firms: the total factor productivity of VC-backed firms in the 5 years preceding the first round of venture capital is 7% higher than similar firms that have not obtained venture capital. The study also supports the idea that venture capital generates value for the invested company. In fact, in the 4 years following the VC investment, the total factor productivity of companies that have obtained venture capital is 5% higher than the productivity of firms that have not obtained venture capital. Moreover, VC-backed firms show a further 7% increase in productivity over the subsequent 5 years. The positive effects on total factor productivity are essentially attributable to sales growth and are much stronger for companies that obtained venture capital from highly reputable VCs.

As for Europe, a study published in the *Journal of Business Venturing* in 2013 by Croce and colleagues using the matching methodology shows a positive treatment effect generated by VCs on the total factor productivity of European startups similar to those that characterize US companies. In fact, for companies that have obtained venture capital, there is a 15% increase in the total factor productivity in the post-investment period compared to their twins. This effect materializes in the first 2 years after the entry of the VC and persists even after the VC has exited the invested company. However, unlike in the US, there is no positive selection effect in Europe. In other words, in the period before the investment, the total factor productivity of VC-backed firms is not higher than that of firms, in which VCs have not invested.

5.3.1 *Summary*

* VC-backed companies, generally, show better economic performance than non VC-backed ones. This effect may be driven by VCs' capabilities in adding value to their portfolio companies (treatment effect) or it is simply because VCs invest in companies that perform better in the first place (selection effect).
* There are two methods available to disentangle those two effects: the matching methodology, where VC-backed firms are compared with similar firms that have not received venture capital, and the use of instrumental variables that are variables positively correlated with the probability to obtain VC, but are not correlated with the firm's economic performance.
* Scientific studies show that in the US, VC-backed firms performs better both before and after the receipt of VC investment, while in Europe, we see a positive treatment effect of VCs on their invested companies, but not any selection effect.

Self-assessment Questionnaire

5.7 Describe the treatment and the selection effect of VCs on their invested companies.

5.8 What are the differences between the US and the European markets in terms of VCs' impact on startups? What may be the drivers of those differences?

5.4 Corporate Venture Capital

Corporate venture capital (CVC) is the investment of corporate funds, i.e. funds provided by non-financial companies, directly in young privately owned companies. Intel Capital is a good example of a CVC. It is a subsidiary of Intel, the world leader in semiconductors that is based in London, which is systematically among the top 10 VC investors worldwide. Google Ventures, a subsidiary of Google, is another example, more recently born.

The aim of this section is to understand the following: (i) what are the objectives pursued by companies that invest in CVC and why some companies do so while others do not, (ii) which structure corporations give to their CVC activities, (iii) what factors make CVC attractive for startups and what are the costs and risks associated with it, (iv) what effects CVC has on the economic performance of invested companies and to what extent these effects differ from the effects of IVCs.

5.4.1 *CVC objectives and organization*

Three factors characterize all CVC investments: (1) Companies that invest in CVC have strategic objectives in addition to financial objectives. These objectives include opening a technology window that allows the parent company of the CVC to monitor the technologies, products or services that the target firm is developing. In this perspective, CVCs can be considered as a fundamental element of the open innovation strategies of large, R&D-intensive companies. Another strategic objective that a company often pursues through its CVC investments is the acquisition of a real option in the target company. At a later period, this option may turn into the acquisition of the target company itself or may benefit the parent company in licensing the technologies developed by the target company. (2) The target companies of CVC investments are privately owned, i.e. they are unlisted, independent and remain so after the CVC investment. (3) CVCs always make minority investments.

CVCs can organize their governance and operations in different ways: (1) A company can act simply as a limited partner. In this case, the company does not directly make CVC investments, but provides its financial resources to an IVC firm, which selects and manages the investments. (2) The company can create a dedicated VC fund in collaboration with other investors. This is the case, for example, of Sequoia Capital, a joint venture between the IVC Sequoia Capital and Cisco Systems. (3) CVC investments can be made directly by a company through its operating business units. (4) A company can make its own CVC investments by creating a wholly owned subsidiary specializing in that activity. This is the case of Novartis Venture Funds and Intel Capital, which are completely owned by Novartis and Intel, respectively, and have a corporate organization separate from that of the parent company. The latter case describes the most widespread organization for CVC activities today, which has some advantages: (1) An independent subsidiary from the parent company looks more like an IVC firm. It is easier for the parent company to design efficient incentives for investment managers than for a business unit within the organization of the company itself. (2) For autonomous CVC subsidiaries, it is easier to join syndicates led by IVC and co-investing with them, exploiting the IVC contacts and investment experience. (3) The risks related to the misappropriation of the knowledge developed by the target investment firms, which we describe in detail in Section 5.4.2, are more limited since contact with the parent company's staff is indirect. In this way, CVCs can incentivize target startups worried about misappropriation of their technology to accept an investment offer.

Even where CVC activities are delegated to an independent company, its degree of autonomy from the parent corporation may be different. In some cases, the parent company reserves the right to authorize each individual investment. In other cases, the level of autonomy available to CVC subsidiaries is significantly higher. They receive funds from the parent company, which they can manage independently without the need for formal prior approval of each investment. Another aspect relates to the reporting mechanisms between the parent company and the CVC managers. Once again, the situations are varied. In a minority of cases, the CVC manager reports directly to the Chief Executive Officer, i.e. the CVC manager is himself a frontline manager. A more frequent situation is the reporting to a front line, which may be the Chief Financial Officer, the Director of Corporate Development or the Director of Acquisitions and Mergers, or a technical manager such as the Chief Technology Officer, the Chief Information Officer or the Head of Research and Development.

5.4.2 *Drivers of CVC Investments*

We now analyze the factors that drive corporations to invest in CVC and which companies are attractive targets for such investments. The scientific evidence regarding the US market suggests that the most attractive companies for CVC investments operate in sectors that are characterized by high technological ferment such as biotechnologies, nanomaterials or the Internet of Things (IOT), in which the complementary assets to the new technologies developed by those companies are a fundamental element to obtain a lasting competitive advantage. In fact, assets, such as sale channels, sale force, product testing skills, supplier networks or the brand, are typically owned by large incumbent companies, which dedicate CVC activities to combine those assets with the innovative technologies developed by the target companies of their investments.

Industrial companies that are more oriented to invest in CVC activities generally have high internal cash flows and, more importantly, the ability to absorb the technological knowledge developed by the target companies thanks to their investments in research and development. In line that, they also have unique complementary assets, especially in the commercial field, which can be placed at the service of the invested companies.

So, what are the advantages of obtaining a CVC investment for a high-technology company? On the one hand, these investors offer target companies coaching capabilities similar to those of IVCs. On the other hand, the CVC investment signals the quality of the target company to less informed third parties, facilitating access to additional resources both financial and not financial.

Finally, as mentioned, the target company obtains privileged access to the unique complementary assets owned by the investor's parent company, with which it can establish a symbiotic relationship that generates significant benefits for both parties.

However, for target companies, CVC investments also have a major disadvantage compared to IVC. They expose the startups to considerable **misappropriation risks** by the corporate investor of the technological knowledge they developed, a situation described in the scientific literature as "swimming with the sharks" syndrome. Clearly, not all sharks are equally dangerous. The problem is that corporate investors, who generate the highest risks of misappropriation, are also those whose parent companies have the most valuable complementary assets for the target companies themselves. Consequently, CVC bonds that could generate high value for the target company may not be realized if the latter fears high risks of misappropriation of its technological knowledge. These risks are clearly greater if the regime of appropriability of the technological knowledge in the sector, in which the target company operates, is weak and if the corporate investor's parent company is a direct competitor of the invested startup.

Dushnitsky and Shaver, in a work published in 2009 in the *Strategic Management Journal*, describe this situation in the US CVC market. They distinguish the biotechnology, pharmaceutical, chemical and medical instrument sectors, where the intellectual property protection regime is strong, from the remaining sectors, where it is weak. In these latter sectors, high technology has a very low probability of accepting investment offers from a corporate investor, whose parent company is a competitor of the startup. This probability is much higher when the sector in which the target company operates is characterized by a strict appropriation regime, because the risks of misappropriation of technological knowledge are more limited.

Nevertheless, there are other defenses that can be used by high technology to protect their technological know-how from corporate investors in a sector where the legal defenses of technological knowledge are ineffective, and therefore the target company could be exploited of the benefits it can get from a CVC investment by a potentially dangerous shark. There are essentially two roads. The first is to use the **time defenses** and postpone the CVC investment to a later round, when the technologies developed by the target company are in a more advanced stage of development and the company is already known by customers. A second way is to use the **social defenses** provided by a highly reputable IVC investor. These investors are an important source of deal flow for corporate investors. Furthermore, they occupy a central position in the network consisting of syndicated investments between VCs and are able to widely advertise any opportunistic behavior of corporate investors against the target companies in their portfolio. Consequently, for CVCs, the opportunity cost of such behavior, in terms of lower future investment opportunities, increases considerably.

A final consideration concerns the European CVC market. In Europe, the syndicated network between investors is fragmented into a series of national networks, few of which are connected. Furthermore, IVCs have greater risk aversion and are less inclined to invest in the seed stage. As a result, the time defenses and the social defenses are much less effective than in the US. In the absence of other opportunities, European startups are more oriented than US ones to swim even at earlier stages of their lifecycle with dangerous sharks.

5.4.3 *The impact of CVC on startups' performance*

We now analyze what the effects are of CVC investments on the economic performance of invested companies and to what extent these effects differ from those of the investments made by IVCs. Determining the impact of CVCs is not an easy task as there is not much public information available. Thus, we primarily rely on the empirical evidence gathered on the topic.

The evidence on these issues generated by scientific studies is not extensive. In a pioneering paper published in 1998, two Harvard economists, Gompers and Lerner, analyze the effects on the start-ups' economic performance of 30,000 venture capital investments made between 1983 and 1994 in the US. The performance measure they considered was the realization of a successful exit through an IPO or an acquisition characterized by a high valuation of the target company. CVC investments do not appear to have significantly different effects from investments made by IVCs. However, CVC investments show heterogeneous effects depending on the strategic fit between the investor's parent company and the target company of the investment. When the strategic fit is high, the economic performance of the invested companies is even higher than that of the target companies of the investments made by IVCs. On the contrary, in the absence of a strategic fit, the economic performance of the target companies of the CVC investment is modest.

A more recent study by Ivanov and Xie (2010) confirms this. In the study, they consider more than 1,500 companies invested by venture capitalists who carried out an IPO in the period 1981–2000. In this case, the performance measure used is the valuation of the target company at the time of the IPO. The authors find that CVC-backed companies have a higher IPO valuation than companies invested by IVCs, but only when there is a high strategic fit between the parent company of the CVC and the target company.

Clearly, the corporate investors with whom a target company has the highest strategic fit are its competitors. The abovementioned evidence therefore illustrates a paradoxical situation. CVCs, whose parent company is a competitor of the target company, entail the highest misappropriation risk of the technological knowledge of the target company itself. For this reason, target companies generally avoid them. However, when such ties are made, they are also the ones that generate the maximum benefits for the target company, in terms of exit success, thanks to the high strategic fit between the target company and the corporate investor.

A more recent study published by Colombo and Murtinu in 2017 extends these analyses to the European case. It provides an accurate comparison of the effects of CVC investments with those made by IVCs, using as a performance measure the total factor productivity, i.e. an index of the economic efficiency of the target companies of the investment. The study also analyzes the dynamics of these effects and the channels through which they manifest themselves, distinguishing between the increase in sales for the same use of production factors — capital and labor— and the reduction in the intensity of use of production factors for the same level of sales. Finally, it considers the effects of investments made by mixed syndicates composed of both CVCs and IVCs. To this end, the study analyzes 215 companies invested by IVCs, 44 companies invested by CVCs, of which 18 received their first round of investment from a mixed syndicate, and 243 twin companies that did not obtain any kind of venture capital investment. Let us initially consider startups invested by IVCs, CVCs and mixed syndicates. In the first two cases, there is a significant increase in the total factor productivity in the period following the investment, which is extremely modest when the investment is made by a mixed syndicate.

More specifically, the treatment effect of investments made by CVCs on the total factor productivity is an increase of 50% compared to the same indicator for twin companies that did not obtain venture capital. This value is very similar to the 41% increase recorded for investments made by IVCs. In both cases, this effect is driven by the sharp increase in sales: +58% in the case of corporate investments and +67% in the case of investments made by IVCs. However, while the positive effect of IVC investments materializes immediately after the investment, the positive effect of CVC investments is slower and only manifests itself from the third year onward.

Another important difference concerns the increase in the number of employees of the invested companies, which is positive and equal to about +20% in the case of investments made by IVCs, while it is completely negligible for CVC investments. In the latter case, the symbiotic relationship between the investor and the startup allows the startup to avoid increasing its workforce and instead use the resources and skills of the CVC investor's parent company.

Finally, in the case of investments made by mixed syndicates composed of both CVCs and IVCs, the effects on the total factor

productivity of the target company, both in terms of sales growth
and employees growth, are negligible. One possible explanation is
that the different objectives among corporate and independent
investors create conflicts that balance out the potential benefits for
the target company.

5.4.4 *Summary*

- CVC is the investment of corporate funds, i.e. funds provided by
  non-financial companies, directly in young privately owned
  companies.
- CVCs, generally, make minority investments in high technology
  with the aim of opening a technology window that allows the
  parent company of the CVC to monitor the technologies, products or services that the target firm is developing and possibly
  acquiring the target company in the future.
- CVCs can organize their governance structure in different ways
  with an increasing level of independence from the parent company. They can make investments through a company's internal
  business unit, create a dedicated VC fund in collaboration with
  other investors and create a wholly owned subsidiary specializing in CVC activity or just acting as limited partners of an IVC
  fund.
- CVC investments expose the invested startups to considerable
  misappropriation risks by the corporate investor of the technological knowledge they developed, i.e. the "swimming with the
  sharks" syndrome. Startups can protect themselves using legal,
  timing and social defenses.
- Considering the impact of CVCs on target companies' performance, scientific evidence has shown that CVC-backed companies perform better than IVC-backed companies, only when
  there is a high strategic fit between the parent company of the
  CVC and the target company and in terms of sales growth.
  However, CVCs have lower or null effects in terms of employees'
  growth and when investments are made by syndicates of CVCs
  and IVCs.

Self-assessment Questionnaire

5.9 Describe the strategies that a startup operating in a high-technology sector characterized by poor legal defenses can pursue to reduce the risk of misappropriation of its technology by a powerful CVC.

5.10 Why did most studies find a poor or negligible impact of CVCs on the economic performance of their invested companies?

5.11 *True, false or uncertain*: An industrial corporation, interested in developing a new AI technology, decides to invest directly in an IVC fund focused on the IT sector. This strategy has a double advantage for the company: it limits the risk of misappropriation of target startups' technology, while the company benefits from the IVC expertise in selecting and managing the investments.

5.12 *True, false or uncertain*: It is better (in terms of economic performance) for a high-technology firm to receive an investment by a CVC whose parent company is a competitor of the startup than by a CVC whose parent company operates in a different sector.

5.5 Governmental Venture Capital

At this point, we have understood that startups are subject to high information asymmetries that prevent them, especially those with high innovative content, to access external equity finance efficiently. Banks, venture capitalists, business angels and the development of other alternative financial providers, such as equity crowdfunding platforms, are not always enough for good functioning of the entrepreneurial finance ecosystems. To fill these equity market gaps, the government and other public institutions can promote initiatives and programs with the aim of alleviating the financial constraints that typically characterize startups. In this context, governmental venture capital (GVC), i.e. VC funds controlled by public institutions, such as supranational or national governments or local institutions, is just one type of public intervention.

Indeed, there are several forms of governmental support for startups. On the one hand, there are the so-called **indirect public policies**. Specifically, the policy maker can define an institutional context that makes startup funding more attractive to a private investor, by designing a more favorable legal system and providing tax-based incentives. For example, the policy maker can facilitate the fundraising process of private VC funds, through less restrictive regulations. In the late 1970s, the US government authorized pension funds to provide capital to private VC funds. This has generated an increase in the overall supply of venture capital for startups. As concerns the level of taxation, an important incentive is represented by the taxation on capital gain, that is, the gain realized by the sale of investments in these startups. By reducing the level of taxation on these capital gains, the expected investment return increases and this obviously represents a strong incentive for private financers to invest in these kinds of companies.

On the other hand, there are **direct public policies**. Governments can implement initiatives that envisage, in various forms, the use of public financial resources to directly support the entrepreneurial ecosystem. One measure of this type is represented by loan guarantee schemes. In other words, the government makes guarantee funds available if the startup is unable to repay a bank loan. In this way, it offers more protection from the insolvency risk to the lender, which, in turn, should be more inclined to disburse the loan. A second policy measure is represented by public subsidies for investments in innovation. These measures are not exclusively aimed at startups, but these firms can benefit from them to finance research and development activities. Finally, the policy maker can decide to actively participate in the VC market through governmental venture capital initiatives. In this case, public financial resources are used to directly finance startups or, alternatively, to finance private VC funds, which, in turn, invest in startups.

GVC identifies a series of measures that directly channel public financial resources to the entrepreneurial ecosystem, in order to facilitate the financing of startups and promote the private VC industry. There are many ways to implement these startup support policies, but three main intervention models can be identified:

1. **Government-owned VC fund:** The functioning broadly follows the model of private VC funds. In this case, an investment fund of a defined amount is created, which is made available to a management company to invest in startups. The substantial difference with the private model is that the capital used for the creation of the fund is public, or the majority is public, and public officials take part in the management of the fund.

2. **Hybrid fund:** They are VC funds that raise capital from public and private capital providers. Both types of investors can participate in the management of the fund's investment activities, although in many cases, the management is in the hands of private investors.

3. **Fund of funds:** An investment fund is created using public capital. However, this capital is not invested directly in startups, but in other private VC funds. In this case, the selection of startups and the management of the investment process are completely in the hands of private investment managers.

An example of the first type is In-Q-Tel, a government-owned VC fund supported by the Central Intelligence Agency, in the US, born to finance startups in the information technology sector. An example of a hybrid fund is, instead, the German High-Tech Gründerfonds fund, backed by the German Federal Ministry of Economics, some banks and other important industrial groups. Finally, an example of the fund of funds model is the European Investment Fund, an initiative financed by the European Investment Bank, the European Commission and EU Member States, which invests through targeted financial intermediaries, such as banks, guarantee and leasing companies, microcredit providers and private equity funds.

5.5.1 *Motivations for GVC initiatives*

After having broadly outlined the main types of GVC initiatives, we now examine whether direct public intervention in the venture capital industry is justifiable from an economic point of view. In fact, we must remember that we are considering public resources, which in theory could be used for other purposes, such as to provide welfare services or to reduce taxes.

There are two important conditions which must be valid so that public intervention can be effectively justified. The first condition is that the private supply of startup finance is not actually sufficient. In many countries, private VC firms are important actors for the financing of high technology, but many startups are still unable to access this financing source. Private VC investors in fact avoid financing projects that are still in the seed stage, far from commercialization. Furthermore, they avoid focusing on very uncertain industries, such as industries where the technological standards are not clear yet. Finally, it must be considered that in the VC industry, the geographical dimension is very relevant. Startups operating in peripheral areas, outside main VC hubs, are not very attractive for investors as the costs of monitoring and managing the investment are too high.

The second condition that must exist is that the public officials in charge of evaluating investment proposals are actually able to assess the quality of the startups to be funded. Public intervention must be aimed at supporting startups which, on the one hand, have the potential to generate high private and social returns, but which, on the other hand, are not yet attractive to private investors. If public officials are able to select high-potential startups, the best ones, the fact that a startup receives GVC can be perceived by other potential private investors as a certification of its quality. As a result, we can expect this startup to attract additional funding from these private investors. By virtue of this certification effect, GVC initiatives can therefore help promote the development of the private venture capital industry.

However, it is legitimate to ask whether these two conditions are actually fulfilled. We can say that it is not obvious that public officials will have the ability to select high-potential startups. This may happen due to a lack of specific skills, which are necessary to evaluate projects characterized by high technological complexity, or due to the presence of political interests that can lead to biases in the decision process. Thus, we have said that the goal of GVC is to facilitate the financing of startups and promote the private VC industry. But, what absolutely must not happen when implementing these initiatives is that GVC substitutes private venture capital. For example, suppose that the public investor provides venture capital to startups on much more advantageous terms compared to those offered by a private investor. The consequence would be that private investors would find it difficult to sustain the competition of the public investor. If this happens, the governmental intervention would be absolutely counterproductive, generating a crowding-out effect that could lead to the overall reduction of the private supply of venture capital for all startups in that market.

5.5.2 *The impact of GVC*

We now ask how to assess the success or failure of governmental venture capital programs. To answer this question, it is necessary to make a premise about the goals of these initiatives. In fact, a substantial difference that characterizes GVC with respect to private venture capital is the presence of objectives that are not strictly linked to investment returns, which instead are the main evaluation parameters when assessing the success of private VC investments. On the contrary, governments have broader objectives, such as the development of an entrepreneurial ecosystem that allows startups to receive the capital needed to grow and innovate. Therefore, to assess the effectiveness of GVC programs, it is important to consider a dual perspective: the perspective of the startup that actually benefits from the measure and the perspective of the entrepreneurial ecosystem as a whole.

First, let us start from the analysis of the impact that these initiatives have on startup performance. In particular, we are interested in understanding, from the point of view of an entrepreneur who is looking for external sources of funding, if it is better to receive venture capital from a public investor or a private investor. It is worth remembering that private VC investors are not limited to providing financial resources to startups in their portfolio, but they play a fundamental role in terms of professionalization, in supporting the startup in finding qualified human resources, in improving internal processes and in creating relationships with potential customers and suppliers. It is the so-called coaching, which is therefore provided along with the financial resources to support startup growth.

The studies that dealt with this topic found that the receipt of GVC generally has a limited effect on startup performance, or at least not comparable to the positive effect measured in the case of private VC (e.g. Brander *et al.*, 2015). This applies to various performance measures, such as, for example, turnover or employment growth, innovation rates and the possibility for a startup to go public. When mixed syndicates of public and private investors make the investments, things go better (Brander *et al.*, 2015; Guerini and Quas, 2016).

But what are the reasons behind the underperformance of governmental programs? A particularly accredited explanation is that GVC initiatives have not been particularly effective in monitoring and coaching startups. This is due to some organizational inefficiencies, such as the fact that in many cases, public officials have to follow a very large portfolio of startups, limiting their ability to manage every single investment project in an effective way, or to the fact that usually public officials receive a remuneration that is less linked to investment performance than private ones.

Considering the second perspective, that of the effect of GVC initiatives at the systemic level, the existing studies have highlighted some successful experiences of GVC programs implemented in different countries (Leleux and Surlemont, 2003; Brander *et al.*, 2015; Guerini and Quas, 2016). For example, we can mention the case of the Small Business Investment Company scheme in the US. The program was implemented at the end of the 1950s, and throughout its history, it has financed very successful companies like Apple or Intel. On a systemic level, it has definitely contributed to developing the private VC industry. Another example of a successful initiative is the Yozma program launched in Israel in 1993. The program has favored the inflow of foreign capital through public–private co-investments, allowing the development of a domestic VC market. With the growth of the domestic market, the role of the government declined and Yozma was privatized.

Despite a lot of successful cases like the ones mentioned, there are also negative experiences. For example, in Canada, with the introduction of the Labor Sponsored Venture Capital Corporations program, there has been a reduction in private VC activity (Cumming and MacIntosh, 2006; Brander *et al.*, 2010; Cumming *et al.*, 2017). The reasons for this failure are manifold. One of the main ones is linked to the fact that the program offered financing conditions for startups that were not sustainable for private investors. The private investors, unable to offer the same conditions, have therefore found themselves displaced and have reduced their level of investing activity.

In general, we can conclude that the effectiveness of GVC programs depends on how these programs are implemented. A careful analysis of past experiences allows us to identify some recommendations in this sense. First of all, such programs need to be undertaken only if there is a real failure in the private supply of venture capital. If this condition is valid, the best results of these initiatives, both by observing the performance of the invested startups and at a systemic level, are obtained in cases of strong collaboration between the public investor and the private investor. Another important factor in the design phase is to avoid as much as possible the public investor investing in the best projects at financing conditions that are not sustainable for private operators. An intervention modality that, on the contrary, has led to very satisfying results is the public–private co-investment with an asymmetrical distribution of investment returns, for the benefit of private investors. On the one hand, this modality ensures that the private investor is protected, at least partially, against losses in the event of investment failure. On the other hand, the private investor has the possibility of obtaining a higher share of returns in case of success. In this way, startups, which otherwise would have been considered too risky by private VCs, manage to attract sufficient financial resources.

5.5.3 *Summary*

- To fill the equity market gap left by private financial providers, the government and other public institutions promote initiatives and programs with the aim to remove the financial constraints of startups.

- One form of this direct intervention is governmental venture capital (GVC), the use of public financial resources to directly support the entrepreneurial ecosystem, facilitate the financing of startups and promote the private VC industry.
- Three main GVC intervention models can be classified as government-owned VC funds, hybrid funds and fund of funds.
- There are two important conditions, which must be valid so that public intervention can be justified. The private supply of startup finance must be insufficient and public officials in charge of evaluating investment proposals must be actually able to assess the quality of the startups to be funded.
- Moreover, to assess the effectiveness of GVC programs, which have completely different objectives compared to private VC, we must consider a dual perspective: the startup and the entrepreneurial ecosystem as a whole.
- GVC generally has a limited effect on startup performance, except in cases of strong collaboration between the public investor and the private investor. Considering the effect of GVC at a systemic level, there has been both positive and negative evidence. Anyway, it is clear that the public should avoid investing in the best projects at financing conditions that may crowd out private VC supply.

Self-assessment Questionnaire

5.13 When is a direct public intervention in the venture capital industry justifiable from an economic point of view?

5.14 What are the circumstances under which GVC programs appear to have the greatest effect on the target companies of their investments and the whole VC market?

5.15 *True, false or uncertain:* The investment returns of GVC funds are a good indicator to measure GVC program success.

5.6 Business Angels

Business angels (BAs), also called informal venture capital investors, are private individuals, who are passionate about a startup, who finance and help the entrepreneur by bringing to the table, in addition to the capital, their own experience, knowledge and network of contacts. Unlike venture capital funds, BAs invests their own capital and their motivation to support a business project may not be exclusively financial (i.e. gaining an economic return on the investment).

While the propensity of private individuals to finance high-risk ventures dates back centuries, the word "angel" being used to characterize the funding practice of private investors derives from Broadway Theater productions, where it was used to identify wealthy individuals who supplied funds for theater productions that would otherwise have had to shut down.

In the early 1980s, William Wetzel (1981a,b, 1983), then a professor at the University of New Hampshire and founder of the university Center for Venture Research, introduced the term "angel" after completing a pioneering study on how entrepreneurs raised seed capital in the US from high-net-worth individuals.

5.6.1 *The characteristics of BAs*

One of the most well-known definitions of business angel was given by Mason and Harrison (2008, p. 309), two English central scholars for business angel research:

> **Business angel:** A high-net-worth individual, acting alone or in a formal or informal syndicate, who invests his or her own money directly in an unquoted business in which there is no family connection and who, after making the investment, generally takes an active involvement in the business, for example, as an advisor or member of the board of directors.

That is, BAs are individuals with high availability of personal funds, who make their own investment decisions to support startups with which they do not have any type of connection in exchange for (usually) a minority share. Typically, BAs are men (on average less than 20% are female investors) between 45 and 55 years of age. They usually have entrepreneurial experience and a considerable network of contacts.

They mostly invest in the very early stages of a company's life, in companies in high-technology sectors, mostly located in places close to their homes.

It is important to distinguish between investments made by these external individuals and those made by family and friends. Here, we do not consider the latter as business angels. According to Mason and Harrison (2008), relatives and friends base their investment decisions on other criteria and considerations than those of professional external investors and, therefore, family-related investments should be excluded from the definition of angel investments.

The previous definition also highlights that BAs can act individually or through syndicates and networks. Recently, there has been a significant increase in investments made by BAs who organize in more or less formal syndicates with other individuals. Individual business angels typically invest between $20,000 and $100,000 of personal funds, while, when acting in syndicates with other individuals, the average investment provided to a startup can increase to an amount between €200,000 and €1 million.

Another important characteristic of BAs is that they tend to have a broad professional experience in the sector in which they invest. This allows them to provide value added to investee companies. They are in fact defined as hands-on investors, i.e. investors who are active in the management of the company and whose contribution is not limited to financial resources. The capital provided by the BAs is also called smart money, as their contribution includes experience in the sector and the network of contacts they have.

Despite some general features, informal investors are highly heterogeneous and empirical studies have tried to categorize them according to various profiles and dimensions. These include, among others, background and competence, investment activity, investment preferences and goals, and type and intensity of their involvement in the startups in which they invest (e.g. Gaston, 1989; Freer *et al.*, 1994; Stevenson and Coveney, 1994; Sørheim and Landstrom, 2001).

However, the categorizations made in some of those earlier studies are based on the assumption that informal investors have static investment behavior, when business angels can actually exhibit different investment patterns over time and from one investment to another, depending on the project characteristics and their own financial situation (see Avdeitchikova, 2008; Lahti, 2011).

For example, Lahti (2011) classifies BAs' investment into four clusters according to their preferred strategy for managing investment risk, based on the comprehensiveness of the due diligence and the level of their post-investment involvement, as shown in Figure 5.3:

1. **Gambles:** Low comprehensiveness of due diligence (1) and low post-investment involvement (2). BAs place limited emphasis on managing risks, both up front and after the investment decision.

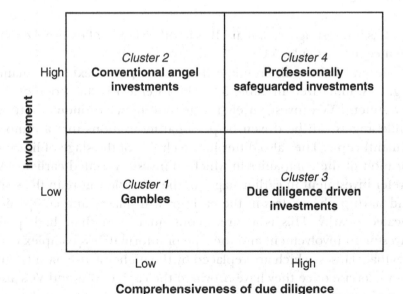

Figure 5.3: Types of business angels (adapted from Lahti, 2011).

This approach to investing might be partly due to BAs' unfamiliarity with the industry sector of the investment and may thus reflect their lack of competence.

2. **Conventional investments:** Low comprehensiveness of due diligence (1) and relatively high post-investment involvement (3). BAs compensate for the low level of due diligence by gaining control after investment through active involvement.

3. **Due diligence-driven investments:** High comprehensiveness of due diligence (4) and low post-investment involvement (1). The focus is on due diligence rather than active involvement. Information asymmetries are reduced *ex ante* to ensure that funds are not addressed to investment opportunities lacking sufficient quality. This is the investment strategy most similar to the one of VCs.

4. **Professionally safeguarded investments:** High comprehensiveness of due diligence (4) and high post-investment involvement (4). This approach is advisable when the degree of uncertainty involved is substantial. It is the least frequent strategy adopted by BAs.

It is interesting to compare BAs to other forms of external equity finance, in particular VCs.

Several factors differentiate these two types of external financing, as summarized in Table 5.3. The foremost is the scope of the investment: VCs invest purely for generating an economic return, while angels can be driven by personal motivations that are more philanthropic. They also differ in the choice of the stage of life and location of the companies in which to invest. As stated earlier, BAs prefer investment in earlier stages of the lifecycle (more in the seed and startup phases, less in the early-growth phase) and companies located nearby. This is a direct consequence of their high post-investment involvement and the type of informal, less complex contractual clauses, which are replaced by the higher active monitoring they exercise once they have provided the capital. BAs and VCs also differ in terms of investment selection and the relevance of the due diligence phase, which are more informal than the respective phases

Table 5.3:   BAs' vs. VCs' characteristics.

	Business angels	VC firms
Definition	Wealthy, well-connected individuals who put their own money in startups with which they do not have personal connections	Professional, specialized investors who use funds raised from other investors (i.e. limited partners of the fund)
Portfolio companies' stage	Seed or startup	Early-growth or growth stage
Portfolio companies' location	Close to their residence	National or international investments
Investment scope	Financial and non-financial objectives	Financial gain
Investment selection	Simple (more complex for BA networks)	Complex and articulated (e.g. pre-screening, screening, due diligence)
Due diligence	Informal	Formal
Post-investment commitment	High	Low
Type of contracts	Simple	Complex
Type of monitoring	Active and informal	Regulated through complex contract clauses
Investment horizon	Long	Short (depending on the life of the fund)

performed by VCs (except for investments made by business angel networks or syndicates, for which these activities are more similar to those of VCs).

Finally, BAs and VCs have different investment horizons. BAs are generally more patient investors than VCs (with an investing holding period even greater than 10 years), whose reasons are mainly linked to factors other than economic performance.

What, in summary, characterizes angel investments with respect to VCs (but also with respect to bank debt), is the fact that BAs use their personal experience to evaluate the project in which they invest, they support the startup in which they invest and they have no pressure to exit the investment within a set period of time.

Further, the relationship between BAs and VCs is worth mentioning. In general, they are considered complementary forms of financing: having different skills and investing according to different logics, they represent a possible heterogeneous combination of resources from which companies can benefit. From another point of view, however, their differences make them two forms of alternative financing that offer companies distinct growth patterns that are not easily reconciled in the same company (Hellman and Thiele, 2015).

However, it is interesting to note that, in terms of aggregate invested amounts, the two forms of financing are rather aligned, while, in terms of number of investments, BAs' deals are far superior to VCs' deals.

5.6.2 *The BA market*

The main business angel markets are Europe and the United States.

Compared to overseas investors, BAs in Europe invest less capital, have longer investment horizons, are more risk-prone and have higher returns.

More recently, BAs have become increasingly relevant as a form of external financing for startups in emerging economies as well, in particular in China and Southeast Asia. In this context, the political and legal features of the markets (e.g. political uncertainty and corruption, lack of supporting institutions for early-stage investments and worse legal protection mechanisms for minority shareholders) influence BAs' profiles and investment practices. In particular, BAs tend to adopt different investment strategies, concerning higher levels of informal networking and co-investments. While business angels usually co-invest in advanced economies to reduce financial risk, they do the same in developing countries to handle the high level of economic, legal, monetary, political, and market risk (Scheela *et al.*, 2015).

From a financial market prospective, BAs have an important role in filling regional financial gaps and in stimulating regional economic development. Different studies have identified in BAs (Harrison and Mason, 1991) and, more importantly, business angel networks (BANs) (Mason and Harrison, 1995; Aernoudt, 2004) the key to fill the equity gap left by VCs in seed and early-stage investments and stimulate entrepreneurship at the regional level.

In this respect, a number of policy measures have been addressed to facilitate the development of the angel market and the connection between BAs and entrepreneurs. Some of those include the creation of business incubators, accelerators, labs and matchmaking services at the regional level, the stimulation of syndication through tax relief mechanisms and co-investment schemes, and the creation of BA academies to improve the financial knowledge and investment practices of novice angels and the investment readiness of entrepreneurs.

Finally, it is important to underline how the estimation and the analysis of the BA market suffer from measurement and evaluation problems. BAs constitute, in fact, an "invisible" population: that is, the only data available are those made personally available by the BAs themselves. Furthermore, the available samples may not be representative of the actual population.

5.6.3 *The BA investment process*

The BA investment process differs from that of other equity investors, such as VCs. Compared to VCs, the BA investment process has some specific characteristics (Paul *et al.*, 2007):

1. BAs give more weight to softer factors, such as the entrepreneur competence, experience and passion.
2. BAs give more importance to earlier phases in the investment process, such as the first meeting with the entrepreneur, while for VCs, the later stages of the process are more important, such as due diligence and the negotiation phase.
3. BAs tend to emphasizes personal factors including the relationship between the angel and the entrepreneur and the fit between the investment project and their personal objectives.

In the following paragraphs, we will focus on two relevant aspects of BAs' investment process: the selection criteria and the post-investment activities performed by business angels and their impact on invested companies and exit performance.

5.6.3.1 *BAs' investment selection criteria*

There are several factors a BA takes into account in selecting her investments: the founder's human capital (i.e. in terms of skills, passion and commitment made in the project), the market potential of the project and the business model of the specific project (i.e. in terms of clarity, ability to attract additional capital and scalability, or ability to modify the scale according to new needs and availability). Another relevant aspect is the fit between the investor and the specific project: about 60% of rejections in the pre-screening phase are linked to poor fit with the investor's interests. Finally, the innovativeness of the project always plays a fundamental role in business angels' investments.

The selection criteria also vary according to the stage of the evaluation process. In the initial phase of the process, the most tangible and objective aspects play a fundamental role. In the later stages of the evaluation process, intangible and subjective aspects, such as those linked to the entrepreneur's passion and commitment, as well as the trust and empathy established between the investor and the entrepreneur, become more relevant.

Furthermore, in the initial selection phase, BAs tend to follow a "heuristic" approach based on the "fatal flaw" principle, i.e. projects are rejected at the first defect identified by the BA in terms of one of the relevant aspects accounted for in the selection process (e.g. technological opportunities, route to market, entrepreneur experience or financial plan) (Maxwell *et al.*, 2011).

5.6.3.2 *BAs' post-investment and performance*

We said that BAs are hands-on investors, which means they become highly involved in the company after the investment.

BAs perform different value-added activities: they provide assistance in everyday operations solving operational problems, they provide advice and mentoring to the entrepreneurs and take part in the Board of Directors or Advisors. BAs also help provide credibility and validation to the venture and, for this reason, facilitate additional funding.

Considering the performance of the companies in which they have invested, BAs are associated with a positive impact in terms of higher survival rates and higher probability of a successful exit (for example, through trade sale or IPO). They also contribute to higher growth rates of employment and increased patenting activity of their portfolio firms.

However, there is also evidence of an opposite result: companies invested by business angels do not experience more successful IPOs (i.e. first quotations on public stock markets) than companies that do not receive this type of financing, while other studies show contrasting results in terms of companies' ability to access subsequent financing after business angel investment.

Finally, considering BAs' investment returns, empirical research has shown that BAs' investments have a large variance in their returns and a negatively distorted distribution with many losses and few, extraordinary high profits.

5.6.4 *BA groups and networks*

In this paragraph, we focus on the formation of groups and networks of BAs, an increasingly important phenomenon in the context of BA financing.

The business angel market is, in fact, characterized by a growing tendency of BAs to invest in syndicates with other individuals and not only individually.

Compared to the investments made individually, the **BA groups** typically invest in companies in more advanced stages of life, apply more complex contractual forms and have an approach more similar to that of professional investors in the way they select projects to invest in. For example, a group of business angels provides for a pre-screening phase of investment opportunities, which is normally carried out by the coordinators of the group itself. The projects that pass the pre-screening phase are submitted to the business angels of the group, who can freely choose to invest or not. Often, the investment is made only if a predefined capital threshold is reached that the business angels undertake to pay. The advantages of joining a coordinated group of business angels are linked to the opportunity cost of the time saved in the pre-screening phase, the reduction of transaction costs and the possibility of pooling the capital and sharing the investment risks.

As a rule, typically, members of a group pay a membership fee (between €250 and €700/year). In a few cases, a success fee (between 3% and 5%) can also be applied to entrepreneurs; however, this is quite infrequent.

Besides the BA groups, there is another reality of syndicated investments between different individuals: the **BA networks**. A BAN is a network of non-professional investors, whose aim is to encourage a meeting between new entrepreneurs, who have just started a startup, and investors interested in investing part of their personal resources in these new business propositions.

There are different networks of BAs at the national level (e.g. IBAN, UK Business Angels Association and Hellenic Business Angel Network) and the supranational level, such as EBAN (European Business Angel Network).

Unlike networks, in groups, BAs commit themselves to pooling their resources in shared investments. The groups therefore allow a consortium for each investment deal and foresee a collaboration on a daily basis with the professional staff of the group, who takes care of pre-selecting the investments to be submitted to the members of the group. It is quite common that one angel (or more), who has invested a significant amount of money, leads each consortium. This lead investor follows the investment at each step, making himself available to the entrepreneur and also watches over the protection of interests of the other business angels who have decided to invest in the company and on the quality of the operation.

5.6.5 *Summary*

- BAs are individuals with high availability of personal funds, who make their own investment decisions to support startups with which they have no personal connection.
- Typically, BAs are men (on average less than 20% are female investors) between 45 and 55 years of age. They have entrepreneurial experience and a considerable network of contacts.
- BAs mostly invest in the very early stages of a company's life, in companies in high-technology sectors and that are located in places close to their homes.
- Compared to other types of equity investors (e.g. VCs), in their investment process, BAs give more weight to softer factors, such as the entrepreneur's competence, experience and passion.
- BAs also give more importance to earlier phases in the investment process, such as the first meeting with the entrepreneur, and emphasize personal factors, such as the fit between the investment project and their personal objectives.
- The current BA market is evolving and is characterized by a growing tendency of BAs to invest through different forms of formal and informal syndicates, such as BA groups and networks.
- Compared to the investments made by individual angels, groups of BAs typically invest higher average amounts of money in companies in more advanced stages of life, apply more complex contractual forms and have an approach more similar to that of professional investors in their selection and investing process.

Self-assessment Questionnaire

5.16 Describe the main differences between BAs and VCs.

5.17 Why are angels an important financial channel for startups before receiving VC investment?

5.18 What are the advantages of organizing groups and networks of BAs? What does it imply for potential target startups? Is it always an advantage for these companies?

5.19 *True, false or uncertain*: We know that BAs are more numerous than VCs; however, we can never know their actual number and investment activity.

5.7 Crowdfunding

5.7.1 *Crowdfunding models*

Crowdfunding is an innovative instrument of entrepreneurial finance, which has its roots in history. A well-known case is related to the construction of the Statue of Liberty, donated by the French to the United States of America, as a sign of friendship between the two countries for the centenary of the Declaration of Independence. The statue, that the chroniclers of the time say was transported by sea in small boxes, was delivered, of course, without the pedestal. In those years, the municipality of New York did not have sufficient financial resources to build the base of the statue. The solution was advanced by Joseph Pulitzer, who on the pages of *New York World* launched a campaign to raise public funds. He asked the citizens of New York to contribute with small donations to the construction of the pedestal of the statue. According to many, this is one of the first examples of crowdfunding in modern history.

Thanks to the spread of the Internet, compared to anecdotal cases in history, crowdfunding has become a popular form of financing increasingly used by entrepreneurs. This form of financing consists of collecting financial resources and feedback from a crowd of participants who voluntarily decide to join a call published on a web platform, typically through small payments, in exchange for some form of remuneration or as a donation (Butticè *et al.*, 2018).

> **Crowdfunding:** Collection of financial resources and feedback from a crowd of participants who voluntarily decide to join a call published on a web platform, typically through small payments, in exchange for some form of remuneration or as a donation.

This definition focuses on two fundamental aspects: (1) It highlights crowdfunding as a way of collecting not only financial resources but also feedback that can be used by the entrepreneurs to improve their business plan and business model (Di Pietro *et al.*, 2018). (2) The definition focuses on the actors involved in a crowdfunding campaign. Unlike other fundraising methods, such as venture capital funds or business angels, crowdfunding requires the presence of an intermediary. This is the **crowdfunding platform**, which acts as a market maker, i.e. a third party that allows the matching of supply and demand for capital. Usually, a crowdfunding platform is a website, on which campaign proponents publish their crowdfunding campaign, for a limited period of time, and on which interested backers can contribute. Thus, thanks to the crowdfunding platform, the campaign proponent, i.e. the entrepreneur who launches the crowdfunding campaign for fundraising, has the possibility to interact with backers, who can provide financial resources to the entrepreneur. The platforms manage the search engines, check the legal requirements, provide online payment mechanisms and, in some cases, perform an initial screening aimed to filter out low-quality campaigns. The number of crowdfunding platforms has grown exponentially over the years, especially in large countries characterized by high national entrepreneurial rates (Dushnitsky *et al.*, 2016); however, a few platforms cover a large majority of the international market.

Crowdfunding is generally divided into four models, depending on the type of remuneration offered to the contributors (Hemer, 2011). In this respect, a distinction is typically made between *donation-based* crowdfunding, reward-based crowdfunding, lending-based crowdfunding and equity-based crowdfunding. On average, equity crowdfunding allows collecting a large amount of capital, compared to the other crowdfunding models, as indicated in Figure 5.4.

The model based on **donation** does not involve any remuneration in return for the donors' contribution.

In the reward-based model, backers contribute in exchange for a product, gadget or service. Sometimes, the reward is simply symbolic (e.g. "An expression of gratitude from the entrepreneur"). In other cases, the reward involves the pre-purchase of a product or

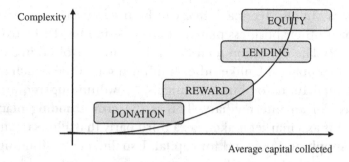

Figure 5.4: Crowdfunding models (adapted from Hemer, 2011).

service (Thürridl and Kamleitner, 2016). Usually, entrepreneurs offer different versions of the product/service associated with different expected contributions to increase the overall crowd participation in the crowdfunding campaign (Buttice and Noonan, 2019). Typically, in donation-based crowdfunding, the average capital collected is limited to a few thousand dollars. **Reward-based crowdfunding** is gaining increasing popularity among entrepreneurs and is typically used to finance projects in the cultural and creative fields (Boeuf *et al.*, 2014). Compared to the donation-based model, reward-based crowdfunding implies superior complexity for proponents. First, in reward-based crowdfunding, proponents are required to include additional information about their campaigns (e.g. related to the reward offered). Second, reward-based crowdfunding requires proponents to organize the production and shipping of the rewards, once the campaign is closed (Tuo *et al.*, 2019). A third crowdfunding model is **lending-based crowdfunding**. In this case, entrepreneurs require the participation of lenders in the form of loans, in most of the cases unsecured. The interest rate offered by the entrepreneur is flexible and typically regulated by an algorithm that considers a credit scoring or competitive pricing (Morse, 2015). Sometimes, in lending-based crowdfunding, the crowd subscribes for securities in a fund which makes the loans to individual borrowers or bundles of borrowers. Finally, in **equity-based crowdfunding**, investors contribute in return for a share of the startup's risk capital. In this case, the investors acquire ownership rights, with the intention of participating in the distribution of future profits. Often, equity crowdfunding campaigns offer voting rights for the crowd, despite this not being mandatory. This crowdfunding model is highly regulated due to its high-risk profile (Giudici, 2015). Moreover, equity crowdfunding implies significant complexity to design and manage the campaign compared to the reward-based model, since it requires an entrepreneur to file a few (mostly unaudited) documents to offer equity online and to provide a comparatively larger set of information to potential investors. Equity crowdfunding has evolved into different business models, among which the nominee structure and the direct ownership are the most diffused (Wright *et al.*, 2017) (Figure 5.5). In direct ownership equity crowdfunding, there is no intermediary and the company reports to each member of the crowd that participated in the campaign, i.e. crowd investors are direct shareholders in the company. On the contrary, in nominee equity crowdfunding, a business vehicle is created ad hoc to administer the shares as the legal representative of the crowd. With the nominee shareholder structure, shareholders benefit from a coordinated effort to monitor and enforce their rights. In terms of economic benefits, with the nominee structure, investors maintain the right to participate in dividend

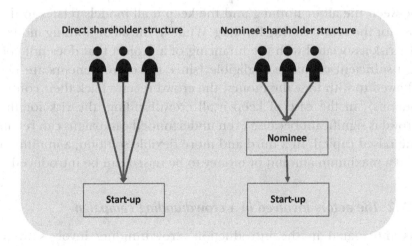

Figure 5.5:   Direct vs. nominee shareholder structure.

distribution and keep the fiscal advantages (e.g. tax reliefs) related to their investment. At the same time, under this structure, firms do not have to manage the administration of their crowd investors on their own, such as organizing large corporate events, or worry about the attendance quorum at general meetings (Cumming and Johan, 2019). One major pitfall of the nominee shareholder structure relates to the firms' limited possibility to reach out to their investors for advice, networking and mentoring (Dharwadkar *et al.*, 2000). Research has demonstrated that, compared to the direct share-holder structure, receiving equity crowdfunding through the nomi-nee shareholder structure facilitates the reception of VC follow-on financing (Butticè *et al.*, 2020).

Another important taxonomy used in crowdfunding relates to the money collection scheme (Cumming and Johan, 2013), and dis-tinguishes between the "all or nothing" and the "keep it all" models. In the **all or nothing model**, the entrepreneur is allowed to withdraw the money collected from the crowd only if a predetermined thresh-old, called funding goal, is reached. On the contrary, in the **keep it all model**, entrepreneurs can cash in the money collected in any case. On average, the all or nothing scheme helps entrepreneurs collect money for risky projects and allows them to collect a greater amount of capital compared to the keep it all model. An important difference between the all or nothing and the keep it all models relates to the risk for the crowd during funding. While in the all or nothing model, the risk associated with the financing of a project that does not col-lect sufficient capital is negligible (since the entrepreneurs are not allowed to withdraw the money, the crowd receive back their contri-butions), in the case of keep it all crowdfunding, the risk for the crowd is significant because even underfunded campaigns can retain the raised capital. In a third and more flexible solution, a minimum and a maximum amount of money to be raised can be introduced.

5.7.2 *The actors involved in a crowdfunding campaign*

As anticipated in the introduction, crowdfunding involves three kinds of players: the proponents, the crowdfunders and the crowd-funding platform.

Proponents are those who launch a crowdfunding campaign seeking financing (Mollick, 2014). Proponents are not necessarily entrepreneurs. Indeed, no-profit entities, private individuals, artists and established firms may also seek funding for the financing of a specific one-off project. Proponents typically use crowdfunding to overcome a funding gap (Brem *et al.*, 2017). Crowdfunding is indeed considered by proponents to be an easy, safe and *well-organized* way to raise money and thus it is extremely valuable for those who can hardly obtain funds from banks, VCs or BAs (Gerber and Hui, 2013; Kim and Hann, 2014; Mollick, 2014; Mollick and Kuppuswamy, 2014).

Proponents are typically male (Mollick and Kuppuswamy, 2014), although in some industries (e.g. fashion) the use of crowdfunding among males and females is evenly split (Greenberg and Mollick, 2017). Moreover, proponents often come from geographical areas where VC investments are limited (Sorenson *et al.*, 2016). Allegedly, proponents leverage their early customers' base when launching a crowdfunding campaign, because they are likely to be the early investors (Giudici and Rossi-Lamastra, 2018).

Backers, also referred to as investors or crowdfunders, are those who support the crowdfunding campaigns by providing financial backing to the projects. Recent studies have shown that many backers interact with proponents during and after the crowdfunding campaign. While some backers restrict interaction to inquire about product delivery or even do not have any interaction with the entrepreneur after the campaign, others offer feedback about the product (Belleflamme *et al.*, 2014) that can allow proponents to anticipate problems and enhance future versions of the product (Colombo *et al.*, 2015). Among backers, some even take an active role during the product design phase (Stanko and Henard, 2017) and are occasionally granted advisory board positions in the crowdfunded firm (Walthoff-Borm *et al.*, 2018). Often, backer involvement in product development is favored by proponents themselves, who offer the possibility for backers to participate in product co-design as a reward in their crowdfunding campaigns (Butticè and Noonan, 2019).

Backers participate in a crowdfunding campaign for multiple reasons. Some backers sustain a crowdfunding campaign driven by the will of obtaining an economic return or a reward. Others contribute to a crowdfunding campaign because they are driven by a strong sense of altruism and a desire to help others (Agrawal *et al.*, 2014; Giudici *et al.*, 2018). Despite altruism and philanthropism being particularly important in donation-based crowdfunding, interviews with crowdfunders indicate that this motivation is compelling in other crowdfunding models as well, especially when support is sought by fundraisers with whom the crowdfunders feel they have some connections or homophilous affinities (Hemer, 2011; Giudici *et al.*, 2020) and when support is sought for social causes that are perceived to be aligned with the crowdfunders' own identity (Gerber and Hui, 2013). Finally, a third group of backers participate in a crowdfunding campaign to obtain social recognition. These crowdfunders envisage crowdfunding as a way to obtain reputational gains (Agrawal *et al.*, 2014, Burtch *et al.*, 2015) for being in an elite league of pioneer early adopters of a new product or a new technology (Hemer, 2011). Many individuals operate both as proponents and backers of different projects and there are even self-ruled open calls for successful fundraisers to become active backers of other fundraisers. For instance, the "Kicking it Forward" Initiative launched on reward-based platforms invites fundraisers to put 5% of their finished product's profits back into other projects (Butticè *et al.*, 2018).

In the case of equity crowdfunding and lending-based crowdfunding, the main objective is to earn a profit from the investment. Equity investors discount the fact that the risk of the investee company may be relevant, but they hope to have found the next Google, Amazon or Tesla. In such a case, they will earn a relevant profit; otherwise, the loss will not significantly affect their wealth ("lottery effect", see Giudici, 2015).

Crowdfunding platforms are intermediaries that work to enable the transactions between the fundraisers and the crowdfunders. These intermediaries serve as matchmakers among proponents and backers. Typically, platforms' revenues are based on a fee on the capital collected by proponents (Burkett, 2011; Koch and Cheng, 2016). For platforms implementing an all or nothing model, the fee is typically charged only on campaigns that have reached their funding goal. Platforms often perform an initial screening aimed to filter out low-quality projects (Löher, 2017). In so doing, they reduce search costs (Agrawal *et al.*, 2014) and coordination costs (Crosetto and Regner, 2018) between the fundraiser and the crowdfunders, lowering the potential for opportunistic behavior associated with a project (Löher, 2017).

5.7.3 *The benefits of crowdfunding for entrepreneurs*

Besides a clear financial advantage, i.e. it can allow the entrepreneur to raise the financial resources needed to develop the business project, crowdfunding implies a number of important non-monetary benefits.

Crowdfunding can be used by an entrepreneur to validate the business idea (Gerber *et al.*, 2013). Indeed, the crowdfunding campaign and its outcome will provide the entrepreneur with an indication of the market response to the business idea. This will allow the entrepreneur to modify the product or the business model, making it more interesting for the market, in case the reaction had not been positive (Brown *et al.*, 2016; Da Cruz, 2018). Crowdfunding also proves useful for marketing purposes, since launching a successful crowdfunding campaign allows fundraisers to gain public attention and increases the public awareness around the project (Gerber and Hui, 2013). At the same time, crowdfunding campaigns, especially successful ones, can serve as a means to help fundraisers achieve legitimacy in the eyes of other investors (Frydrych *et al.*, 2014; Colombo and Shafi, 2019). In the case of reward-based crowdfunding, the launch of a crowdfunding campaign can also constitute a market study. Indeed, information from the campaign can be used to assess market demand for a new product, through the offering, as a reward, of the product associated with different required pledges during the campaign. Moreover, the possibility of offering the product as a reward in a reward-based crowdfunding campaign allows the entrepreneur to exploit crowdfunding to sell on the crowdfunding platform products for which traditional markets are difficult to penetrate.

Another prominent benefit associated with crowdfunding relates to the aggregation of a community around the entrepreneurial project (Butticè *et al.*, 2017). Indeed, by launching a campaign, crowdfunding allows campaign proponents to aggregate a group of backers who pursue a common goal, feel they have a positive and measurable impact on the final output, develop emotional connections to the project and have frequent interactions with the core members of the project. Occasionally, this group of backers can have interactions with the entrepreneur with the goal of improving product design. Feedback by these backers typically highlights defects, suggests product improvements and provides ideas to reduce production time and costs (Di Pietro, 2018). Contrary to expectations, it has been shown that the crowd provides feedback not only in reward-based and donation-based campaigns but also in equity-based ones.

5.7.4 *The risks of crowdfunding for entrepreneurs*

Aside from the aforementioned advantages, crowdfunding also has a number of disadvantages that a wise entrepreneur should take into account.

First, because crowdfunding involves the launch of a public call for funding, it obliges the entrepreneur to disclose information on a web platform, thus making potentially accessible to a broad audience sensitive information about the product and the business model (Ahlers *et al.*, 2015). The disclosure of this information raises the risk of product counterfeiting and reduce fundraisers' ability to appropriate the innovation value (Roma *et al.*, 2018; Stanko and Hennard, 2018), because of unintended knowledge misappropriation. In aiming to provide enough information to convince potential backers to finance the project (i.e. to reduce information asymmetries), the disclosure of information may also reduce a firm's competitive advantage, if strategic information, that can be used by competitors to improve their own performance, practices and processes, is made available (Gleasure, 2015).

Crowdfunding also involves reputational risks if the entrepreneurs have not been able to raise sufficient financial resources.

Since the information about failed campaigns remains public, crowdfunding entails the risk of social stigma for fundraisers unable to attract enough financial resources (Gerber and Hui, 2013). The loss of reputation may reduce entrepreneurs' ability to obtain funds in the future both through crowdfunding campaigns (Butticè *et al.*, 2017) and from professional investors (Roma *et al.*, 2018; Signori and Vismara, 2018).

Finally, crowdfunding involves the aggregation of a community of financiers who interact with the entrepreneur. While, as mentioned above, this can be an advantage for the entrepreneur who obtains feedback to improve the product, it also involves greater management and coordination efforts that must be counted among the potential disadvantages of crowdfunding. The management of the crowd has been reported by the literature as a costly activity that takes time, energy and effort (Giudici, 2015; Butticè and Noonan 2019) and may ultimately result in additional challenges during the production (da Cruz, 2018) and in delays in the delivery of products (Mollick, 2014). Since the crowd typically provides diverging feedback and suggestions about product development (Stanko and Hennard, 2017), crowdfunding also raises an additional challenge for entrepreneurs. Indeed, if entrepreneurs attempt to include all diverging feedback in product development, the final product quality may be negatively affected (Butticè and Noonan, 2019). Finally, in the case of equity crowdfunding, the presence of a wide number of funders may curb professional investors when considering a future follow-up investment in the company, because they will have to bargain with many unsophisticated shareholders to reach an agreement (Giudici, 2015). To this extent, nominee structures (see Section 5.7.2) may be helpful to solve the problem (Table 5.4).

5.7.5 *How to run a successful crowdfunding campaign*

A crucial aspect that has been explored in the scientific literature on crowdfunding is the design choices to create a successful campaign.

But, what is a successful crowdfunding campaign? Typically, success in crowdfunding is inherently related to financial success: the

Table 5.4: Crowdfunding advantages vs. disadvantages.

Crowdfunding

Advantages	Disadvantages
• Access to finance	• Misappropriation
• Idea validation	• Counterfeiting
• Public attention	• Loss of competitive advantage
• Means to achieve legitimacy	• Loss of reputation
• Marketing means	• Coordination effort to manage the
• Creation of a community which provides feedback and sustains product development	community
	• Potential problem for follow-up VC rounds

ability of the campaign to reach the financing target set by the entrepreneur. However, in some cases, this measure has also been accompanied by indicators to quantify feedback from funders. Between these indicators, we take into account the number of backers in the campaign and the number of textual comments sent by backers on the campaign page. Unless otherwise indicated, the results that will be presented below refer to financial success, i.e. the achievement of the funding target.

We can broadly classify the determinants of crowdfunding success into three major categories: (a) campaign characteristics, (b) proponent characteristics and (c) backers' characteristics (Figure 5.6).

Campaign characteristics refer to the design choices of the crowdfunding campaigns and are related to how the campaign appears on the crowdfunding platform to backers. Among campaign characteristics, a crucial decision relates to the duration of the campaign. The scientific literature has shown that a very long campaign duration significantly reduces the likelihood of funding because of the informative value of this choice (Mollick, 2014). A proponent who decides to launch a very long campaign suggests to the market a lack of confidence in his/her business project, and for this reason he/she defines a wide time window for collecting a sufficient amount of funds. The strongly negative interpretation of this choice by the market reduces the probability that the campaign

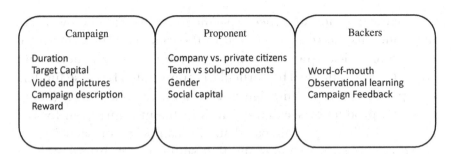

Campaign	Proponent	Backers
Duration Target Capital Video and pictures Campaign description Reward	Company vs. private citizens Team vs solo-proponents Gender Social capital	Word-of-mouth Observational learning Campaign Feedback

Figure 5.6: Determinants of crowdfunding success.

will achieve success. On major reward-based crowdfunding platforms, the duration of the campaign is typically one month, while on
lending- and equity-based platforms, the duration is typically
longer.

Another relevant campaign design choice relates to the funding
target. Campaigns with a higher target capital have more difficulty
in achieving success (Colombo *et al.*, 2015). Aside from the clearly
inherent difficulty of raising sufficient funding to achieve a higher
target, this result is again explained by the informative value of this
decision. Indeed, the choice to use crowdfunding for raising particularly large amounts of finance is interpreted by investors as an
indication that the entrepreneur has not been able to obtain financing from other forms of financing. The reference is clearly to VC
funds and BAs, who are typically investors commonly involved in the
financing of large business projects.

It is clear that a key theme for a successful campaign is the
reduction of information asymmetries, in order to reduce the tendency of backers to infer indications on the quality of the business
project from decision-making not necessarily related to this. In this
sense, it is essential for those who want to launch a crowdfunding
campaign to provide information on the quality of the business project that can be used by a wide audience. The literature has shown
that providing this information, which can be conveyed in different
forms, such as videos, images, graphics or text descriptions, increases
the chances of success of the campaign (Butticè and Colombo,
2020).

Finally, another key aspect, specific to reward-based crowdfunding, concerns the rewards offered in the campaign. In a successful campaign, typically two types of rewards are offered: material and symbolic. The latter will be particularly appreciated by those funders who participate in a campaign not for an economic return (i.e. to receive a product or seeking for an investment return) but for the pleasure of having participated in the campaign or of being an active member of a community that supports an entrepreneurial project. Symbolic rewards will therefore be crucial for the involvement of these funders. Widely used symbolic rewards are the inclusion in a wall of fame or public recognition for support (e.g. in film credits or on the proponent's social media pages).

As anticipated earlier, the success of the crowdfunding campaign also depends on proponent characteristics. In many platforms, crowdfunding campaigns can be launched by both companies and private citizens. As a matter of fact, companies show a higher success rate in comparison to individuals since companies are perceived to be less risky by potential backers. Scholars also compared the success rates of campaigns submitted by teams and individual entrepreneurs. It has been shown that entrepreneurial teams are more likely to succeed, particularly when they can demonstrate cohesiveness, motivation and complementarity of skills. It has been shown that campaigns with at least one woman in the team perform better than projects that have only men in the team. The former have higher success rates and attract more female backers, especially in the case of technological projects (Greenberg and Mollick, 2017). This dynamic is also confirmed in equity crowdfunding (Vismara *et al.*, 2016). Finally, a crucial aspect highlighted in the literature concerns the so-called social capital of the entrepreneur, in the sociological sense of the term, i.e. networks, norms and social trust that facilitate coordination and cooperation for mutual benefit (Putnam, 1995, p. 1). It has been shown that a proponent's social capital facilitates success (Butticè *et al.*, 2017; Colombo *et al.*, 2015). Typically, two different facets of social capital are important for crowdfunding success. These are external and internal social capitals depending on whether the social capital was developed outside rather than inside the crowdfunding platform. Both external and internal social capitals are positively associated with campaign success. But how can a proponent accumulate social capital in a crowdfunding platform? One possibility for proponents is to provide financing to other campaigns on the same platform before the launch of their own campaign (Colombo *et al.*, 2015). Another possibility for serial proponents, i.e. proponents who launch multiple campaigns, is to accumulate internal social capital by launching prior successful campaigns (Butticè *et al.*, 2017). Also, this form of internal social capital helps the fundraiser achieve funding, but the effect is short-lived and disappears quickly.

Finally, coming to backers, it has been widely shown that backers who back a project early facilitate the attraction of further contributions (Colombo *et al.*, 2015) and work as a predictor that reduces the information asymmetries surrounding the campaign (Burtch *et al.*, 2013). This effect could be explained by at least three different mechanisms: observational learning, word of mouth and uncertainty reduction through extensive feedback (Colombo *et al.*, 2015). Observational learning occurs when the crowdfunders are unclear regarding the quality of a project and take the observation of large support from others as a signal of confidence in the project quality. Next, early crowdfunders facilitate word of mouth (Vismara, 2016) by sharing the crowdfunding campaign information via social media (Mollick, 2014). Finally, early backers allow proponents to improve their campaign design by providing suggestions and feedback, which ultimately allow proponents to target a broader audience (Colombo *et al.*, 2015).

5.7.6 *Data on crowdfunding in Europe and in the world*

Crowdfunding is a method of financing that appeared in the second decade of the 2000s and has shown particularly high growth rates over the years.

A study commissioned by the World Bank has shown that in 2012, 3 years after the birth of this mode of collection, campaigns around the world raised almost $2.7 billion. After 3 years, in 2015, the total volume of funding amounted to $34.4 million, more than 12 times the value of the previous 3 years. Based on this early boom, it was expected that crowdfunding would have allowed startups to raise $100 billion by 2025. Compared to these very optimistic estimates, crowdfunding has partly lost its traction. However, it remains a relevant source of financing for entrepreneurs.

Among the crowdfunding models, historically, lending-based crowdfunding has always been the most widespread method of fundraising.

The second-most diffused crowdfunding model is donation-based crowdfunding. However, over the years there has been a steady decline in the relative share of this form of financing. On the contrary, there has been growth in both the reward-based crowdfunding market, primarily due to the growth of the US market, and in equity crowdfunding driven by growth in the European market.

According to the latest estimates in a study commissioned by the European Community, the European market grew from €1.13 billion in 2013 to €5.43 billion in 2015. From 2016 to 2017, volumes raised by crowdfunding increased from €7.67 billion to €10.44 billion.

This result, although particularly positive, contrasts with much more pronounced growth in North America (+248%) and the Asia-Pacific region (+366%). In other words, crowdfunding in Europe is growing significantly, but at a slower pace compared to other regions. Looking at the differences between European countries, the spread of crowdfunding shows a strong imbalance in geographical terms, with the United Kingdom representing about 80% of the total continental market. This gap was exacerbated in recent years, as the UK market has had higher growth rates than the rest of Europe. In continental Europe, the countries where crowdfunding is most widespread are France, with about 5.9% of the EU total and about 31.3% of the total for continental Europe, followed by Germany, with a market corresponding to 4.6% of the EU total and 24.4% of the total for continental Europe, and the countries of northern Europe.

In Europe, as in the rest of the world, lending-based crowdfunding (either to businesses or individuals) is the main model and represents about 60% of the total funding raised. However, country-level information shows that there is a substantial variation, from 22% in Spain to 90% in the Scandinavian countries. Equity crowdfunding represents about 16% of the total crowdfunding market. This is well above the global average. This is due to a greater regulatory effort in European countries, which has made it possible to collect equity capital through crowdfunding well before the rest of the world.

As mentioned, compared to the European context, the evolution of the crowdfunding market in the rest of the world shows some differences. In addition to the differences in growth rates already highlighted, crowdfunding in the rest of the world is considerably larger. China is the world's largest market for crowdfunding. In terms of total volume, the Asia-Pacific region is about 17 times larger than Europe and more than twice as large as the American region.

Another substantial difference between Europe and the rest of the world is the spread of the reward-based model, particularly widespread in the United States, which hosts the 5 largest crowdfunding platforms of this type in the world. Finally, the last distinction concerns the average size of the crowdfunding campaign launched in Europe compared to the rest of the world. The literature has shown that crowdfunding campaigns launched in Europe have on average lower collection targets than the rest of the world. This evidence has been confirmed both by aggregated data analysis and by analyzing the data for each crowdfunding model.

Research has shown that the development of crowdfunding in different countries is widely influenced by country-level characteristics. More advanced regulations for businesses or simpler procedures to run a business are positively associated with the size of the national crowdfunding market. Similarly, it has been shown that crowdfunding is influenced by country-level cultural differences. Indeed, crowdfunding markets are larger in countries characterized by a higher level of individualism, i.e. countries where the ties among individuals are loose.

5.7.7 *Summary*

- Crowdfunding consists of the collection of financial resources and feedback from a crowd of participants who voluntarily decide to join a call published on a web platform, typically through small payments, in exchange for some form of remuneration or as a donation.
- There are 4 different types of crowdfunding: donation, reward, lending and equity.
- Crowdfunding platforms serve as matchmakers among proponents and backers, i.e. they are intermediaries that work to enable the transactions between the fundraisers and the crowdfunders.
- In addition to fundraising, crowdfunding allow entrepreneurs to validate the business idea, collect feedback to improve the product and raise public awareness on the entrepreneurial project.
- However, crowdfunding also entails a number of pitfalls, including misappropriation risks and costs associated with the management of the crowd after the campaign
- The success of a crowdfunding campaign depends on the design of the campaign, the proponent's characteristics and on the ability to attract a large number of backers in the early phases of the fundraising.

Self-assessment Questionnaire

5.20 Describe the role of crowdfunding platforms. Does their role change in equity-based crowdfunding?

5.21 According to the different phases of the company's lifecycle, when does crowdfunding signify as a valuable financial source to collect external funds for startups and companies?

5.22 *True, false or uncertain*: VCs always prefer financing startups that received equity crowdfunding.

5.23 *True, false or uncertain*: Success of a crowdfunding campaign depends solely on proponents' characteristics.

References

Agrawal, A., Catalini, C., & Goldfarb, A. (2014). Some simple economics of crowdfunding. *Innovation Policy and the Economy, 1*, 63–97.

Ahlers, G. K., Cumming, D., Günther, C., & Schweizer, D. (2015). Signaling in equity crowdfunding. *Entrepreneurship Theory and Practice, 39*(4), 955–980.

Aernoudt, R. (2004). Incubators: Tool for entrepreneurship? *Small Business Economics, 23*(2), 127–135.

Avdeitchikova, S. (2008). On the structure of the informal venture capital market in Sweden: developing investment roles. *Venture Capital, 10*(1), 55–85.

Belleflamme, P., Lambert, T., & Schwienbacher, A. (2014). Crowdfunding: Tapping the right crowd. *Journal of Business Venturing, 5*, 585–609.

Boeuf, B., Darveau, J., & Legoux, R. (2014). Financing creativity: Crowdfunding as a new approach for theatre projects. *International Journal of Arts Management, 16*(3), 33–48.

Brander, J. A., Du, Q., & Hellmann, T. (2015). The effects of government-sponsored venture capital: international evidence. *Review of Finance, 19*(2), 571–618.

Brander, J. A., Egan, E., & Hellmann, T. (2010) Government sponsored versus private venture capital: Canadian evidence. In: J. Lerner and A. Schoar (eds.), *International Differences in Entrepreneurship, National Bureau of Economic Research,* University of Chicago Press, Chicago, 275–320.

Brem, A., Bilgram, V., & Marchuk, A. (2019). How crowdfunding platforms change the nature of user innovation–from problem solving to entrepreneurship. *Technological Forecasting and Social Change, 144,* 348–360.

Brown, R., Mawson, S., & Rowe, A. (2019). Startups, entrepreneurial networks and equity crowdfunding: A processual perspective. *Industrial Marketing Management, 80,* 115–125.

Burkett, E. (2011). A crowdfunding exemption-online investment crowdfunding and US secrutiies regulation. *Transactions: Tenn. J. Bus. L., 13,* 63.

Burtch, G., Ghose, A., Wattal, S. (2015). The hidden cost of accommodating crowdfunder privacy preferences: A randomized field experiment. *Management Science, 5*(2069), 949–962.

Butticè, V., & Colombo, M. G. (2020). Crowdfunding for entrepreneurs. In *Oxford Research Encyclopedia of Business and Management.*

Butticè, V., & Noonan, D. (2020). Active backers, product commercialisation and product quality after a crowdfunding campaign: A comparison between first-time and repeated entrepreneurs. *International Small Business Journal, 38*(2), 111–134.

Butticè, V., Colombo, M. G., & Wright, M. (2017). Serial crowdfunding, social capital, and project success. *Entrepreneurship Theory and Practice, 41*(2), 183–207.

Butticè, V., Franzoni, C., Rossi-Lamastra, C., & Rovelli, P. (2018). *The Road to Crowdfunding Success: A Review of Extant Literature*, Oxford University Press.

Chemmanur, T. J., Krishnan, K., & Nandy, D. K. (2011). How does venture capital financing improve efficiency in private firms? A look beneath the surface. *The Review of Financial Studies, 24*(12), 4037–4090.

Colombo, M. G. & Murtinu, S. (2017). Venture capital investments in Europe and portfolio firms' economic performance: Independent versus corporate investors. *Journal of Economics & Management Strategy, 26*(1), 35–66.

Colombo, M. G., & Shafi, K. (2019). Receiving external equity following successfully crowdfunded technological projects: An informational mechanism. *Small Business Economics*, 1–23.

Colombo, M. G., Franzoni, C., & Rossi-Lamastra, C. (2015). Internal social capital and the attraction of early contributions in crowdfunding. *Entrepreneurship Theory and Practice, 39*(1), 75–100.

Croce, A., Martí, J., & Murtinu, S. (2013). The impact of venture capital on the productivity growth of European entrepreneurial firms: "Screening" or "value added" effect? *Journal of Business Venturing, 28*(4), 489–510.

Crosetto, P., & Regner, T. (2018). It's never too late: Funding dynamics and self pledges in reward-based crowdfunding. *Research Policy, 47*(8), 1463–1477.

Cumming, D., & Johan, S. (2013). Demand-driven securities regulation: evidence from crowdfunding. *Venture Capital, 15*(4), 361–379.

Cumming, D. J., & Johan, S. A. (2019). *Crowdfunding: Fundamental Cases, Facts, and Insights*, Academic Press.

Cumming, D. J., & MacIntosh, J. G. (2006). Crowding out private equity: Canadian evidence. *Journal of Business Venturing, 21*(5), 569–609.

Cumming, D. J., Grilli, L., & Murtinu, S. (2017). Governmental and independent venture capital investments in Europe: A firm-level performance analysis. *Journal of corporate Finance, 42*, 439–459.

Da Cruz, J. V. (2018). Beyond financing: Crowdfunding as an informational mechanism. *Journal of Business Venturing, 33*(3), 371–393.

Da Rin, M., Hellmann, T., & Puri, M. (2013). A survey of venture capital research. In *Handbook of the Economics of Finance*, 2, 573–648. Elsevier.

Dharwadkar, B., George, G., & Brandes, P. (2000). Privatization in emerging economies: An agency theory perspective. *Academy of Management Review, 25*(3), 650–669.

Di Pietro, F., Prencipe, A., & Majchrzak, A. (2018). Crowd equity investors: An underutilized asset for open innovation in startups. *California Management Review, 60*(2), 43–70.

Dushnitsky, G., Guerini, M., Piva, E., & Rossi-Lamastra, C. (2016). Crowdfunding in Europe: Determinants of platform creation across countries. *California Management Review, 58*(2), 44–71.

Dushnitsky, G., & Shaver, J. M. (2009). Limitations to interorganizational knowledge acquisition: The Paradox of Corporate Venture Capital. *Strategic Management Journal, 30*(10), 1045–1064.

Freear, J., Sohl, J. E., & Wetzel Jr., W. E. (1994). Angels and non-angels: Are there differences? *Journal of Business Venturing*, 9(2), 109–123.

Frydrych, D., Bock, A. J., Kinder, T., & Koeck, B. (2014). Exploring entrepreneurial legitimacy in reward-based crowdfunding. *Venture Capital, 16*(3), 247–269.

Gaston, R. J. (1989). *Finding Private Venture Capital for Young Firm: A Complete Guide*, New York: Wiley.

Gompers, P., & Lerner, J. (1998). Venture capital distributions: Short-run and long-run reactions. *The Journal of Finance, 53*(6), 2161–2183.

Guerini, M., & Quas, A. (2016). Governmental venture capital in Europe: Screening and certification. *Journal of Business Venturing, 31*(2), 175–195.

Gerber, E. M., & Hui, J. (2013). Crowdfunding: Motivations and deterrents for participation. *ACM Transactions on Computer-Human Interaction (TOCHI), 20*(6), 1–31.

Giudici, G., (2015). Equity crowdfunding of an entrepreneurial activity. In Audretsch, D., Lehmann, E., Meoli, M. and Vismara, S. (eds.), *University Evolution, Entrepreneurial Activity and Regional Competitiveness*, Springer.

Giudici, G., Guerini, M., & Rossi-Lamastra, C. (2018). Reward-based crowdfunding of entrepreneurial projects: The effect of local altruism and localized social capital on proponents' success. *Small Business Economics, 50*, 307–324.

Giudici, G., Guerini, M., & Rossi-Lamastra, C. (2020). Elective affinities: Exploring the matching between entrepreneurs and investors in equity crowdfunding. *Baltic Journal of Management, Forthcoming.*

Giudici, G., & Rossi-Lamastra, C. (2018). Crowdfunding of SMEs and start-ups: When open investing follows open innovation. In *Researching Open Innovation in SMEs.* Frattini, F., Usman, M., Roijakkers, N., & Vanhaverbeke (Eds.), World Scientific.

Greenberg, J., & Mollick, E. (2017). Activist choice homophily and the crowdfunding of female founders. *Administrative Science Quarterly, 62*(2), 341–374.

Harrison, R. T., & Mason, C. M. (1991). Informal investment networks: A case study from the United Kingdom.

Hellmann T., & Thiele, V. (2015). Friends or foes? The interrelationship between angel and venture capital markets. *Journal of Financial Economics, 115*(3), 639–653.

Hemer, J. (2011). A snapshot on crowdfunding. Available at: https://www.econstor.eu/handle/10419/52302.

Ivanov, V. I., & Xie, F. (2010). Do corporate venture capitalists add value to start-up firms? Evidence from IPOs and acquisitions of VC-backed companies. *Financial Management, 39*(1), 129–152.

Kim, K., & Hann, I. H. (2014). Crowdfunding and the democratization of access to capital: a geographical analysis. Available at: http://papers.ssrn.com/sol3/papers.cfm?abstract_id=2334590.

Koch, J. A., & Cheng, Q. (2016). The role of qualitative success factors in the analysis of crowdfunding success: Evidence from Kickstarter.

Lahti, T. (2011). Categorization of angel investments: An explorative analysis of risk reduction strategies in Finland. *Venture Capital, 13*(1), 49–74.

Leleux, B., & Surlemont, B. (2003). Public versus private venture capital: Seeding or crowding out? A pan-European analysis. *Journal of Business Venturing, 18*(1), 81–104.

Löher, J. (2017). The interaction of equity crowdfunding platforms and ventures: an analysis of the preselection process. *Venture Capital, 19*(1-2), 51–74.

Mason, C. M., & Harrison, R. T. (1995). Closing the regional equity capital gap: The role of informal venture capital. *Small Business Economics, 7*(2), 153–172.

Mason, C. M., & Harrison, R. T. (2008). Measuring business angel investment activity in the United Kingdom: A review of potential data sources. *Venture Capital, 10*(4), 309–330.

Maxwell, A. L., Jeffrey, S. A., & Lévesque, M. (2011). Business angel early stage decision making. *Journal of Business Venturing, 26*(2), 212–225.

Mollick, E. (2014). The dynamics of crowdfunding: An exploratory study. *Journal of Business Venturing, 29*(1), 1–16.

Mollick, E., & Kuppuswamy, V. (2014). After the campaign: Outcomes of crowdfunding. Available at: https://ssrn.com/abstract=2376997.

Morse, A. (2015). Peer-to-peer crowdfunding: Information and the potential for disruption in consumer lending. *Annual Review of Financial Economics, 7,* 463–482.

Paul, S., Whittam, G., & Wyper, J. (2007). Towards a model of the business angel investment process. *Venture Capital, 9*(2), 107–125.

Puri, M., & Zarutskie, R. (2012). On the life cycle dynamics of venture-capital-and non-venture-capital-financed firms. *The Journal of Finance, 67*(6), 2247–2293.

Roma, P., Gal-Or, E., & Chen, R. R. (2018). Reward-based crowdfunding campaigns: Informational value and access to venture capital. *Information Systems Research, 29*(3), 679–697.

Scheela, W., Isidro, E., Jittrapanun, T., & Trang, N. T. T. (2015). Formal and informal venture capital investing in emerging economies in Southeast Asia. *Asia Pacific Journal of Management, 32*(3), 597–617.

Signori, A., & Vismara, S. (2018). Does success bring success? The post-offering lives of equity-crowdfunded firms. *Journal of Corporate Finance, 50,* 575–591.

Sorenson, O., Assenova, V., Li, G.-C., Boada, J., & Fleming, L. (2016). Expand innovation finance via crowdfunding: Crowdfunding attracts venture capital to new regions. *Science, 6319,* 1526–1528.

Sørheim, R., & Landström, H. (2001). Informal investors — A categorization, with policy implications. *Entrepreneurship and Regional Development, 13*(4), 351–370.

Stanko, M. A., & Henard, D. H. (2017). Toward a better understanding of crowdfunding, openness and the consequences for innovation. *Research Policy, 46,* 784–798.

Stevenson, H., & Coveney, P. (1994). *Fallacies Corrected and Six Distinct Types of Angel Identified.* Venture Capital Report, Templeton College Oxford.

Thürridl, C., & Kamleitner, B. (2016). What goes around comes around? *California Management Review, 58*(2), 88–110.

Tuo, G., Feng, Y., & Sarpong, S. (2019). A configurational model of reward-based crowdfunding project characteristics and operational approaches to delivery performance. *Decision Support Systems, 120,* 60–71.

Vismara, S. (2016). Information cascades among investors in equity crowd-funding. *Entrepreneurship Theory and Practice, 42*(3), 467–497.

Walthoff-Borm, X., Vanacker, T. R., & Collewaert, V. (2018). Equity crowd-funding, shareholder structures, and firm performance. *Corporate Governance: An International Review, 26*(5), 314–330.

Wright, M., Siegel, D. S., & Mustar, P. (2017). An emerging ecosystem for student startups. *The Journal of Technology Transfer, 42*(4), 909–922.

Wetzel, Jr., W. E. (1981a). Informal risk capital in New England. In K. H. Vesper (Ed.), *Frontiers of Entrepreneurship Research*, Wellesley, MA: Babson College, pp. 217–245.

Wetzel Jr., W. E. (1981b). Technovation and the informal investor. *Technovation, 1*(1), 15–30.

Wetzel Jr., W. E. (1983). Angels and informal risk capital. *Sloan Management Review, 24*(4), 23–34.

Chapter 6

Startup Valuation

6.1 Introduction

In this chapter, we examine the most common valuation models of a startup. Startup valuation is an important objective, both from a strategic point of view in order to understand the impact of investment choices on business value and from a financial point of view in relation to investors' future returns. Compared to established firms, the valuation of startups is much more complicated since startups are exposed to extreme volatility and risks, and they have almost no track record and often few tangible assets.

There are several valuation models that can be used. First, we can evaluate a startup using an **asset-based valuation** logic, that is, evaluating its individual existing assets. However, this is generally possible if the company holds tangible or financial assets that are easily evaluable: a rare case for a project at the seed stage, for which there is often only an idea and a team.

Alternatively, we can evaluate startups using the **discounted cash flow model (DCF)**. In this case, we have to estimate the capability of a company to generate future cash flows. This is a recommended methodology when the company is going to grow in the future starting today with low or even negative profitability, as is the typical case of many startups. The approach consists of forecasting future operating cash flows, net of cash used for investments and working capital. However, we cannot simply sum up these values, since the

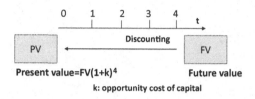

Figure 6.1:   Computation of present value.

money assumes a different value over time. It is not equivalent, in fact, to receive 100 euros today or the next year, because if we receive the money today, we can invest the cash in the market in alternative assets and obtain a capital that is greater after one year. In other words, there is an opportunity cost of capital connected to alternative investments existing in the market. When we have a future cash flow, called FV, for example, at time 4, we need to compute its present value, which is the equivalent value to time 0, dividing it by $(1 + k)$ to the power of 4 (see Figure 6.1).

Furthermore, we cannot be certain that the realized future cash flows will be equal to the estimated ones, and therefore this is considered through the cost of capital. In fact, a greater risk related to the company will require a larger return for investors, in other words, a larger risk premium captured by the cost of capital. Especially when dealing with projects in the startup phase, or even in the seed phase, in high-technology sectors, it is not uncommon to consider an extremely high cost of capital. This is because the probability of failure is very high and investors must target particularly high returns obtained from few projects to compensate for the resources lost in many others.

Figure 6.2 shows what should be the cost of capital required for a startup project. For example, we can see that if the goal is to multiply by 5 the value within 7 years, the annual cost of capital should be at least 26%.

A third commonly used method is the **relative valuation** method, which is based on **multiples of comparable companies** or **comparable transactions** realized on the acquisition market. The main idea

Exit Year for Investment

	1	2	3	4	5	6	7	8	9	10
1.0x	0%	0%	0%	0%	0%	0%	0%	0%	0%	0%
2.0x	100%	41%	26%	19%	15%	12%	10%	9%	8%	7%
3.0x	200%	73%	44%	32%	25%	20%	17%	15%	13%	12%
4.0x	300%	100%	59%	41%	32%	26%	22%	19%	17%	15%
5.0x	400%	124%	71%	50%	38%	31%	26%	22%	20%	17%
6.0x	500%	145%	82%	57%	43%	35%	29%	25%	22%	20%
7.0x	600%	165%	91%	63%	48%	38%	32%	28%	24%	21%
8.0x	700%	183%	100%	68%	52%	41%	35%	30%	26%	23%
9.0x	800%	200%	108%	73%	55%	44%	37%	32%	28%	25%
10.0x	900%	216%	115%	78%	58%	47%	39%	33%	29%	26%

Return Multiple on
Invested Capital

Source: Industry Ventures LLC

Figure 6.2: Cost of capital.

here is to get the market's opinion about the company, by identifying a set of similar companies and then using a number of valuation ratios for these companies in order to arrive at the company valuation. Whereas in the DCF method, we try to predict future cash flows and the target cost of capital, here we avoid relying solely on our own judgment and look at how the public market values similar companies.

Consider the following example (see Figure 6.3).

We want to evaluate company "x" that today has an EBITDA (earnings before interest, taxes, depreciation and amortization) equal to 1 million euros. We have found three comparable companies listed on the stock exchange (with observable share prices) that are similar in terms of sector, size and age. We have collected the EBITDA for the three companies and we can now compare it with the companies' market capitalization (market cap or equity market value, E), which is the market price of shares times the total number of shares outstanding. Suppose for simplicity that these companies are not financed with debt; in this case, their **enterprise value** (EV) corresponds to their **equity value** (E). In this way, we have found that, on average, comparable companies are worth 4.9 times the EBITDA (on average, E/EBITDA=4.9). Thus, we can apply the same multiple to company "x" and evaluate its equity value at 4.9 times its EBITDA.

Current EBITDA of company "x" = € 1 million

Comparable companies listed on stock exchanges:

Company	Current EBITDA	Market capitalization (€)	Multiple E / EBITDA
A	€ 2.0 million	€ 10.0 million	5
B	€ 3.0 million	€ 15.6 million	5.2
C	€ 5.0 million	€ 22.5 million	4.5
Average			4.9

Company "x"value: € 1 million x 4.9 = € 4.9 million

Figure 6.3:   Relative valuation.

A number of multiples can be calculated using other economic performance measures both for the numerator and the denominator. Some of the most used ones are as follows:

1. **EV/EBIT:** EV is the total market value of all securities of the company, including common and preferred stock, long- and short-term debt, and so on. The denominator, EBIT, is often seen as equivalent to a constant-state cash flow indicator, in which case the EV/EBIT ratio can be viewed as the ratio of firm value to cash flow.

2. **EV/EBITDA:** This is also very common. Like EBIT, EBITDA is a proxy of cash flow generation, especially in the short term (until capital expenditures can be postponed to replace depreciated assets).

3. **EV/Revenue:** This multiple seems to be entirely independent of any cash flow measure, as revenues are not an indicator of profitability. Nonetheless, this metric is useful, especially for high-growth sectors, where companies often have negative EBIT and EBITDA, making it impossible to calculate such multiples. Revenues, instead, are always available.

4. **Price/Earnings:** This is one of the most known multiples. Price refers to the price of a single stock and earnings refers to the earnings per share. Thus, we can compute the P/E ratio by dividing the market cap by net income. Because only

shareholders are remunerated through earnings, in the numerator, we consider the market cap, instead of the whole enterprise value.

5. **Price/Book:** In this measure, price of a single stock is divided by the book value per share. The P/B ratio is not linked to cash flow at all. The idea is that a P/B ratio below 1 means that the shareholders will be better off selling their stake (but only if we consider the book value of equity to be accurate).

6. **EV/Employees:** This is similar to the EV/Revenue ratio and has no clear connection to the cash flow. However, the number of employees can be the fastest moving indicator of the growth of a business, and even though the other indices are lagging behind, the EV/Employee may provide some guidance about the future prospects of a company. Of course, it will never be as negative as EV/Revenues.

Finally, a similar approach consists of finding comparable companies that have recently undergone an M&A transaction. If the acquisition value is known, we can, as before, obtain a multiple and apply it to the startup we are considering for investment.

6.2 The VC Method

The VC method is a widely applied methodology, commonly used by VCs to evaluate startups.

This is a very simple model. An example of its application is shown in Figure 6.4. Consider a startup. In the economic-financial projections of its business plan, the management has estimated an EBITDA equal to 1.5 million euros after 5 years from the moment the estimate takes place.

Clearly, this is an objective; there is no certainty on the achievement of such a result, due to the high uncertainty and the high risk attached to the entrepreneurial project. Suppose that to evaluate the startup, we decide to use the relative valuation method. In this case, we can proceed as before, except that we have to estimate the value of the startup at the time of the VC exit; in fact, it is only then

VC evaluation: example	
Expected EBITDA at time 5	€ 1.5 million
Multiple considered	5x
Expected value of company at time 5	5x € 1.5 million = € 7.5 million
Cost of capital k	25%
Value of business today	€ 7.5 million / (1+25%)^5 = € 2.458 million
Assume we need new equity capital to run the business:	
Amount to be raised	€ 1 million
Post-money valuation	€ 2.458 million
Fraction of equity capital to be sold	€ 1 million / € 2.458 million = 40.7%
Pre-money valuation	€ 2.458 million − € 1 million = € 1.458 million

Figure 6.4: VC method application.

that the VC will make its capital gain on the investment. Let us suppose that the exit happens in 5 years.

Suppose also that we adopt an EV/EBITDA multiple equal to 5, computed starting from the EV/EBITDA of a number of comparable companies observed on the public market (ideally, we should also consider the value of the multiples at the time of the VC exit for those comparable companies, i.e. in 5 years). The expected value of the company at exit, in 5 years from now, if everything goes according to plan, will be equal to 7.5 million euros ($=1.5$ million $\times 5$). The next step is to compute the present discounted value of the company today to be compared with the investment made by the VC. Therefore, we have to discount the 7.5 million euro value with the cost of capital, which we assume equal to 25%. The value of the startup today will therefore be about 2.5 million euros.

Now, let us assume that the company needs an investment of 1 million euros to grow. The fraction of the equity capital to be offered to the VC in exchange for the money (1 million euros) can be computed as a simple proportion dividing the amount to be raised by the present discounted value of the company. Thus, we should offer at least 40.7% of the equity capital to get a 1 million euro investment from the VC.

The valuation of 2,458 million euros is called **post-money valuation**, because it reflects the value of the startup if the company manages to collect the money. The difference between the post-money valuation and the money to be raised is called the **pre-money valuation**.

It should be emphasized that the valuation strongly depends on the initial assumptions and on the hypotheses concerning the multiples and the cost of capital. A proper sensitivity analysis is recommended to evaluate how robust the valuation estimate is compared to any change in the initial values of the cost of capital, future cash flow estimates and so on.

6.3 Summary

- There are three main models that can be used to estimate the value of a startup: the asset-based logic method, the discounted cash flow method and the relative valuation method.
- The DCF method consists of forecasting future operating cash flows, net of cash used for investments and working capital, and, then, discounting these cash flows with a proper cost of capital to take into account the opportunity cost of money and the intrinsic risk related to entrepreneurial projects.
- The relative valuation method is based on multiples of comparable companies or comparable transactions realized on the market. The main difference with the DCF consists of using public information available on the stock market to identify a set of similar companies to evaluate the startup.
- The VC method is a very popular and simple valuation technique used by VCs. In this chapter, we showed a practical example of its application.

Self-assessment Questionnaire

6.1 The VC AB is considering a 5 million euro investment in the company YZ. AB estimates an expected exit time of 7 years and an exit valuation of the company of 500 million euros. Considering a cost of capital of 20%, what percentage of the equity capital should YZ offer to AB?

6.2 What is pre-money and post-money valuation?

6.3 How sensitive is the previous investment recommendation to different assumptions about the exit valuation and the cost of capital?

Chapter 7

Incubators

7.1 Introduction

The creation of the first private incubator in New York dates back to 1959, while the first public incubator in Philadelphia was established in 1964. After that, business incubation became widespread during the 1960s and 1970s.

Today, **business incubators** or, more simply, incubators are an integral part of the entrepreneurial ecosystem. Incubators favor the creation and the growth of new businesses by providing assistance to entrepreneurs and startups in obtaining funding, developing the business model and marketing plans, building the business management team and accessing specialized professional services.

Incubators focus on the early stages of new venture development and, for a limited period (on average 3 years), provide incubated startups with tangible resources, such as spaces, shared facilities and administrative services, and intangible resources, such as knowledge and contacts. The startups that enter the incubator are selected on the basis of well-defined criteria that vary from incubator to incubator. Such criteria normally include the feasibility of the business idea and the skills of the entrepreneurs.

Incubators are funded through rents paid by incubated startups. Less frequently, incubators take equity stakes or portions of the income of incubated startups. Moreover, incubators are usually funded by sponsors.

In the literature, several definitions of business incubator have been advanced, as there are many different organizational forms that can help companies set up and grow. Some studies have used this term for similar yet very different concepts, such as science parks (Ratinho and Henriques, 2010) or technology and university research centers (Roig-Tierno *et al.*, 2015).

A central concept of incubators is that they target ventures which are in their early development stages, so the term incubator should not be confused with similar organizations that generally support more mature firms (Bergek and Norrman, 2008).

A good solution is, therefore, to provide a broader and a narrower definition of incubators based on their primary goal (Hausberg and Korreck, 2020, p. 163):

Business-incubating organizations (in the broader sense) are those that support the foundation and/or growth of new businesses as a central element of their organizational goal.

Business Incubators (in the narrower sense) are business-incubating organizations that support the establishment and growth of new businesses with tangible (e.g. space, shared equipment and administrative services) and intangible (e.g. knowledge, network access) resources during a flexible period and are funded by a sponsor (e.g. government or corporation) and/or fund themselves by taking rent (or, less frequently, equity) from incubates.

While the broader definition allows one to include a large universe of business-incubating organizations, the narrower definition allows the distinction of classical incubators from other incubating organization forms, for example, accelerators. Accelerators are specific cohort-based programs providing education and mentoring to startups' teams and connecting them with experienced entrepreneurs, VCs, BAs and corporations, and helping them in the process of fundraising (Cohen 2013; Cohen and Hochberg, 2014; Hochberg, 2016).

7.2 Typologies of Incubators

As mentioned earlier, there are several typologies of incubating organization forms.

Depending on the nature of the sponsor, a first distinction can be made between public incubators and private incubators (Kuratko and LaFollette, 1987).

In Europe, the first and most popular **public incubators** were the BICs, Business Innovation Centers. Their origin dates back to 1984, when the first BICs were set up by the European Commission. BICs are centers of entrepreneurial innovation aimed at promoting the economic development of the regions they belong to, supporting the birth of innovative small and medium enterprises and new job creation. Typically, BICs offer a set of basic incubation services, including the provision of space, infrastructure, communication channels, information on external financing opportunities and visibility. The list of BICs recognized by the European Union is available on the website of the European BIC Network.

Other popular public incubators are **university incubators**. These incubators are set up by universities willing to adopt a direct entrepreneurial role in generating and spreading technological knowledge. University incubators offer two main categories of services: typical incubator services, including physical facilities, business assistance and access to capital, and university-related services, including access to libraries, laboratories and equipment, support for research and development activities, education and training of entrepreneurs and employees, and access to the pool of young graduates.

Finally, public incubators are frequently located within science and technology parks. These are infrastructures linked to public research centers that aim to enhance and develop the economic growth of the geographical areas in which they settle, by favoring dialogue and technological transfer between the world of public research and businesses.

Considering **private incubators**, they help entrepreneurs by providing pre-seed and seed capital traditionally offered by business angels and early-stage VCs. The services offered by private incubators include the efficient completion of the entrepreneurs' business model, validation and vetting, the provision of experienced operation staff, recruiting mechanisms and access to a network of domain experts. Often, private incubators are corporate incubators, i.e. they are created and controlled by large companies. The parent companies of these incubators usually aim to support the rise of new independent business units, the so-called corporate spin-offs, which generally come from internal research projects and are the result of parent companies' diversification strategies. However, besides hosting corporate spin-offs, corporate incubators also host external companies. Finally, there are private incubators set up by individuals or groups of individuals (companies too may be among their founding partners), who invest their own money in startups in exchange for an equity stake.

A particular type of incubating organization is **accelerators**. Starting in 2005, when Y Combinator was founded in Silicon Valley, these new players have spread in the global entrepreneurial ecosystem. Accelerators are support programs for companies that have already begun to move on the market and need seed capital or know-how to move from the startup phase to the mature business phase, with a well-defined position in the market. Usually, accelerators are fixed-term cohort-based programs, with a duration that varies from a few weeks to a year. They provide education, monitoring and mentoring to startup teams or, more rarely, individual entrepreneurs, connecting them with corporate executives and experienced entrepreneurs, who act as mentors, and investors, such as BAs and VC fund managers. Accelerators aim to help startups overcome the organizational, operational and strategic difficulties that may arise during the first period of activity. These programs normally culminate in a public pitch event, during which "accelerated" entrepreneurs present their startups to a large group of potential investors. It is possible to distinguish between independent acceleration programs, public accelerators and corporate acceleration initiatives.

7.3 The Incubation Process

The incubator process starts with the search for and selection of proposals. Maintaining a steady flow of quality proposals is a key success factor for incubators (Patton *et al.*, 2009).

Incubators differ in the criteria and process to decide which startups to accept for entry. In principle, we can between distinguish incubators in which selection is focused primarily on the evaluation of the viability of the idea and its market potential and incubators in which the focus is on the analysis of entrepreneurs' skills and personality (Bergek and Norrman, 2008). In addition to adopting different selection criteria, incubators adopt different selection approaches. Some incubators prefer a "picking-the-winners" approach, which involves applying the selection criteria rigidly, to identify a few potential successful companies *ex ante*. Other incubators prefer a "survival-of-the-fittest" approach, i.e. they apply less rigid selection criteria so as to accept a greater number of startups, and rely on markets to provide the selection processes that over time will separate winners from losers (Bergek and Norrman, 2008).

Moreover, selection criteria may vary for different incubators typologies. In particular, private incubators review potential incubatees more rigorously by applying criteria similar to those applied by VCs (Ford *et al.*, 2010; von Zedtwitz, 2003). Beyond these criteria, corporate incubators consider strategic alignment between their startup portfolio and their parent company as a relevant selection criterion.

The incubation process then differs in the services the incubators offer. In incubators' business models, the supply of spaces has become increasingly secondary, while the business support services provided in various areas, such as sales, accounting, legal support, contracts, patents and strategies, have become increasingly important. Because incubators aim to adapt their services as much as possible to the specific needs of incubated startups, the choice of the startups to incubate affects the mix of services provided and vice versa (Hackett and Dilts, 2004).

There are then various service delivery approaches. Some incubators follow a "strong intervention" approach, i.e. they guide startups through the incubation process. For example, where the entrepreneurial team lacks fundamental skills, the incubator staff imposes training paths on the entrepreneurs or integrates into the entrepreneurial team new members who can bring the missing skills. Other incubators see themselves as facilitators of a process that incubated startups manage independently, and therefore, they provide resources and assistance only at the request of incubated entrepreneurs (Bergek and Norrman, 2008).

Finally, the incubation process differs according to how they perform their mediation role. When incubators do not have the resources required by a startup internally, for example, specialist technical skills, they assist the venture through networking activities (Scillitoe and Chakrabarti, 2010). Some incubators, generally university incubators, are particularly effective in matching incubated entrepreneurs with experts in the technological field, while others, in particular private incubators, are effective in matching incubated entrepreneurs with capital providers and experts in the commercial field.

7.4 Impact on Incubated Startups

Entrepreneurs usually decide whether to apply to an incubator or not considering two fundamental aspects: the specific characteristics of the incubation process and the effects that incubation could have on the development of their own startup. While we analyzed the first aspect in the previous paragraph, we focus here on incubators' potential impact on startup performance.

So far, many scientific studies have tried to evaluate the contribution of incubation to business results by comparing the performances of incubated startups with those of comparable non-incubated startups. Conducting this impact analysis is not easy, because detecting superior performance among incubated startups is not enough to argue that the incubation process has positive effects. As incubators' managers have incentives to identify the startups with greater chances of success, while avoiding weak candidates, the superior performance of incubated startups is (at least in part) the result of superior skills of incubated entrepreneurs or better business ideas. Therefore, to correctly evaluate the contribution of incubation to startup performance, one should show that incubated startups would have been less successful if they had not been incubated.

The scientific literature has revealed that the main impact of incubators consists of creating an effective bridge between incubated startups and public research organizations. Indeed, incubated startups show a greater propensity to collaborate with universities and other public research organizations than comparable non-incubated startups, and more frequently participate in international research and development projects (Colombo and Delmastro, 2002). These collaborations allow incubated startups to access scientific knowledge at the frontier, acquire skills in specific technological fields and use sophisticated instruments and equipment that would not be available to them due to cost reasons. Consequently, although there are no significant differences between incubated and non-incubated startups in terms of innovative activity and survival, it has been shown that incubated startups more frequently adopt advanced technologies and have higher growth rates in the number of employees and, to a lesser extent, in sales (Colombo and Delmastro, 2002; Stokan *et al.*, 2015).

However, the simple access to knowledge developed in the academic field that incubators make possible is not sufficient to stimulate the growth of incubated startups. Collaborations with research organizations translate into higher growth rates only if incubated startups have sufficient absorptive capacity, i.e. they are able to recognize the value of scientific knowledge of academic origin, assimilate it and apply it for commercial purposes. For instance, Schwartz (2013) does not find positive results that incubated firms have higher probability of long-term survival than comparable firms located outside incubators.

In addition to services provided by incubators, such as networking and collaborations, further factors may influence startups' performance. Barbero *et al.* (2012) show that performance varies according to the typology of the incubator. Regional development incubators seem not to be effective, while university incubators perform satisfactorily. Instead, firms incubated in private and basic research incubators show significantly higher performance in terms of firm growth, participation in R&D programs, input and output R&D and employment generation cost.

A second fundamental effect of incubation concerns the access of startups to external financing. Incubators help alleviate the financial constraints that incubated startups experience by helping these firms raise public funding. However, there is no evidence that incubation favors access to venture capital or business angel financing.

7.5 Summary

- Incubators favor the creation and the growth of new businesses by providing assistance to entrepreneurs and startups in obtaining funding, developing the business model and marketing plans, building the business management team and accessing specialized professional services.
- While there are different types of incubators, a central concept is that they target ventures which are in their early development stage.
- Depending on the nature of the sponsor, we can distinguish between public incubators and private incubators.
- University incubators (public) offer university-related services, including access to laboratories and equipment, support for research and development activities, training of entrepreneurs and employees, and access to the pool of young graduates. Instead, private incubators are able to help entrepreneurs by providing pre-seed and seed capital in addition to traditional incubator services.
- Scientific studies have revealed that the main impact of incubators consists of creating an effective bridge between incubated startups and public research organizations. However, collaborations with research organizations translate into higher growth

rates only if incubated startups have sufficient absorptive capacity.

- Another fundamental effect of incubation concerns the access of startups to external financing.

Self-assessment Questionnaire

7.1 Describe the role of business incubators. Do public and private incubators have the same objectives?

7.2 *True, false or uncertain:* For a startup, it is always better to be incubated by a private incubator than by a public incubator.

7.3 *True, false or uncertain:* The only effect of incubators is to create a bridge between incubated startups and public research organizations.

References

Barbero, J. L., Casillas, J. C., Ramos G. A., & Guitar, S. (2012). Revisiting incubation performance: How incubator typology affects results. *Technological Forecasting and Social Change, 79*(5), 888–902.

Bergek, A., & Norrman, C. (2008). Incubator best practice: A framework. *Technovation, 28*(1–2), 20–28.

Cohen, S. (2013). What do accelerators do? Insights from incubators and angels. *Innovations, 8*(3/4), 19–25.

Cohen, S., & Hochberg, Y. V. (2014). Accelerating startups: The seed accelerator phenomenon. Available at SSRN 2418000.

Colombo, M., & Delmastro, M. (2002). How effective are technology incubators? Evidence from Italy. *Research Policy, 31*(7), 1103–1122.

Ford, S., Garnsey, E., & Probert, D. (2010). Evolving corporate entrepreneurship strategy: Technology incubation at Philips. *R&D Management, 40*(1), 81–90.

Hackett, S. M., & Dilts, D. M. (2004). A systematic review of business incubation research. *Journal of Technology Transfer, 29*, 55–82.

Hausberg, J. P. & Korreck, S. (2020). Business incubators and accelerators: a co-citation analysis-based, systematic literature review. *The Journal of Technology Transfer, 45*(1), 151–176.

Hochberg, Y. V. (2016). Accelerating entrepreneurs and ecosystems: The seed accelerator model. *Innovation Policy and the Economy, 16*(1), 25–51.

Kuratko, D. F., & LaFollette, W. R. (1987). Small business incubators for local economic development. *Economic Development Review, 5*(2), 49.

Patton, D., Warren, L., & Bream, D. (2009). Elements that underpin high-tech business incubation processes. *Journal of Technology Transfer, 34*(6), 621–636.

Ratinho, T., & Henriques, E. (2010). The role of science parks and business incubators in converging countries: Evidence from Portugal. *Technovation, 30*(4), 278–290.

Roig-Tierno, N., Alcazar, J., & Ribeiro-Navarrete, S. (2015). Use of infrastructures to support innovative entrepreneurship and business growth. *Journal of Business Research, 68*(11), 2290–2294.

Schwartz, M. (2013). A control group study of incubators' impact to promote firm survival. *Journal of Technology Transfer, 38*(3), 302–331.

Scillitoe, J. L., & Chakrabarti, A. K. (2010). The role of incubator interactions in assisting new ventures. *Technovation, 30*(3), 155–167.

Stokan, E., Thompson, L., & Mahu, R. J. (2015). Testing the differential effect of business incubators on firm growth. *Economic Development Quarterly, 29*(4), 317–327.

von Zedtwitz, M. (2003). Classification and management of incubators: Aligning strategic objectives and competitive scope for new business facilitation. *International Journal Entrepreneurship and Innovation Management, 3*, 176–196.

Glossary

3Fs: Friends, Family and Fools (3Fs). Capital is provided to an early-stage company (typically at the seed stage) by friends and relatives. Fools refers to the fact that investing in a business at such an early stage involves high risks because the venture has a high potential for failure.

Accelerator: A fixed-term cohort-based program providing mentoring to startups' teams and connecting them with experienced entrepreneurs, VCs, BAs and corporations, while helping them in fundraising.

Adverse selection: A market situation where buyers and sellers have different information, i.e. one of them has superior or better knowledge that can be used to gain from the transaction at the expense of the other party.

Agency theory: It explains issues in the relationship between business principals and their agents. Principal–agent problems arise when a person or an entity, the agent, makes decisions in the name and on behalf of another person or entity, the principal. If the decisions taken by the agent differ from those optimal for the principal, the latter will bear a cost, known as the agency cost.

All or nothing: A crowdfunding model in which the entrepreneur can collect the money raised from the crowd only if a predetermined threshold, called funding goal, is reached.

Anchor investors: The first subscribers of a VC fund, who act as catalysts for subsequent investors.

Angel = Business angel

Asset-based analysis: A company valuation methodology, in which the company's market value is estimated based on the market value of its assets.

BA = Acronym for **business angel**.

BA group: An organized group of business angels, where angels commit themselves to pooling their resources in shared investments. The group also performs screening and due diligence activities, reducing the cost connected to investment.

BA network: A non-profit organization promoted by business angels, whose primary aim is to connect entrepreneurs who need funding with individuals interested in investing part of their personal capital.

Backers: In crowdfunding, those who support the crowdfunding campaigns by pledging money to the projects.

Bank-affiliated venture capitalists (BVC): The VC firm under the control of a financial organization, such a bank or insurance company.

BAs = Acronym for **business angels**.

Bootstrapping: A series of methods through which startups can avoid resorting to the external capital market, using the founders' personal funds and organizing their operations in order to minimize financial needs.

Business angel (BA): A wealthy individual who invests in high-technology, high-growth startups. A business angel differs from a venture capitalist because the former uses her own money.

Business incubator: Organizations that support the foundation and/or the early growth of new businesses as a central element of their organizational goal, providing startups with tangible (e.g. space, shared equipment and administrative services) and intangible (e.g. knowledge, network access) resources.

Business plan: A summary document about the business (its technology, market, financial projections) and the management team that entrepreneurs present to potential investors.

Captive venture capitalist: The VC firm under the control of an external organization. The parent organization can be a non-financial corporation (Corporate venture capitalists), a financial institution, such as a bank (Bank-affiliated venture capitalists), or a public entity (Governmental venture capitalists).

Carried interest: The share of the capital gains of a VC fund that is allocated to the general partner. Typically, a fund must return the capital invested by the limited partners plus any preset rate of returns (i.e. hurdle rate) before the general partner can share the profits of the fund.

Charter: A legal document, included in the term sheet, that sets out the main rules of governance between the entrepreneur and the VC investor.

Collateral: Security pledged or promised to a bank or other lender if the repayment of a loan cannot be made, typically tangible assets of a company.

Commercial bank: A type of financial institution, which performs the functions of accepting deposits from the general public and giving loans for investment.

Committed capital: The total amount of capital promised to the fund by the limited partners.

Company lifecycle: The progression of a business and its phases over time. The stages of the lifecycle are seed, startup, early growth, expansion and late stage.

Comparable multiple analysis: A company valuation methodology, in which the company's market value is estimated based on the market values of similar assets (i.e. the ratio comparing the value of a company-specific variable, such as EBITDA or cash flow, is the same across similar companies).

Corporate investor = Corporate venture capitalist

Corporate venture capitalist (CVC): The VC firm under the control of a non-financial organization, such a large industrial corporation.

Type 1 credit rationing: A form of credit rationing that occurs when some specific group of borrowers (i.e. companies) who request a loan cannot fully obtain it.

Type 2 credit rationing: A form of credit rationing that occurs when some specific group of borrowers (i.e. companies) obtains a loan and others do not, although they are completely indistinguishable from each other, even if they are willing to pay a higher interest rate.

Credit rationing: A state of equilibrium, generated by the fully rational optimal response of banks to the existence of the information asymmetries, in which banks limit the amount of loans to borrowers.

Crowdfunding platform: A website acting as a financial intermediary between proponents/startups of crowdfunding campaigns and backers/small investors.

Crowdfunding: A collection of financial resources and feedback from a crowd of participants, who voluntarily decide to join a call published on a web platform (crowdfunding platform), typically through small payments, in exchange for some form of remuneration or as a donation.

Deal flow: The number of potential investments that a VC fund reviews in any given period.

Debt capital market: A type of market where companies raise funds from banks or trading debt securities. Securities include corporate and government bonds. Raising debt capital means that the company borrows funds that have to be paid back together with interests on those funds.

Direct public policy: Use of public financial resources to directly support the entrepreneurial ecosystem.

Discounted cash flow (DCF) analysis: A company valuation methodology, in which the company's market value is estimated as the sum of the discounted value of all cash flows produced by the company in the future.

Donation-based crowdfunding: A crowdfunding model, in which backers do not receive anything in exchange for the money pledged to the project. This is used to support social causes.

Drag-along clauses: A right of some category of shareholders to force other investors to sell their stake in the company.

Drawdown: Capital transferred (part of the committed capital) from the limited partners to the general partners.

Dual track: An exit strategy where investors negotiate with potential buyers for a trade sale while simultaneously filing for the listing process on the stock exchange.

Due diligence: Careful investigation and analysis of all aspects of a potential investment target.

Early-growth stage: The state of a company after the seed and startup stages, but before generating revenue. Typically, a company in the early stage has a core management team and a proven concept or product, but no positive cash flows.

Elevator pitch: A concise presentation, lasting only a few minutes (an elevator ride), by an entrepreneur to a potential investor about an investment opportunity.

Enterprise value: Total market value of all securities of the company (i.e. value of a company available to shareholders, debt holders and other stakeholders).

Entrepreneurial (finance) ecosystem: A local or regional community of entrepreneurs, startups, scientists and financial providers.

Entrepreneurial finance: The study of theories and concepts related to traditional corporate finance applied to the process of making financial decisions in startups.

Equity capital market: A type of market where companies raise funds in exchange for company shares. Raising equity means that a company sells a certain amount of ownership in the company in exchange for cash.

Equity value: Market value of a company's equity (i.e. value of a company available to shareholders). It accounts for all the ownership interest, including the value of unexercised stock options and securities convertible to equity.

Equity-based crowdfunding: A crowdfunding model, in which investors receive a company's share in exchange for the capital invested in an entrepreneurial project.

Equity: The ownership structure of a company represented by common shares and preferred shares. Equity = assets – liabilities.

Exit stage (or just Exit): The plan for generating profits for owners and investors of a company. Typically, the options are to be acquired or to make an initial public offering (IPO).

Expansion phase: The state of a company characterized by a complete management team and a substantial increase in revenue. Typically, a company in the expansion stage has positive cash flows.

Financing round: A financial event where a company receives capital from investors. Financing rounds are often referred to sequentially as first round (= Series A), second round (= Series B), etc.

Follow-on round/investment: An investment made in round Y by a VC that has already invested in the company in round X, where Y is higher than X.

Fund of funds: A private or public VC fund that invests in other private VC funds.

General partner (GP): The investment manager of a limited partnership VC fund.

Government-owned VC fund: A VC fund created with public money or for the most part with public money. The fund is managed by the public investors.

Governmental venture capitalist (GVC): The VC firm under the control of a public organization, such as a national or regional government.

Hurdle rate: A preset rate of returns that the fund must pay to limited partners before the general partner can start to earn any carried interest.

Hybrid VC fund: A VC fund created with public and private money. Both private and public investors participate in the management of the fund.

Incubator = Business incubator

Independent venture capitalist (IVC): The VC firm that is a legal stand-alone company, with the typical structure of a VC fund.

Indirect public policy: Favorable legal framework or tax-based incentives that enhance the supply of private funding for startups.

Information asymmetry: It emerges between two parties involved in a transaction when one party (e.g. the entrepreneur) has more or better information than the other party (e.g. the investor). This asymmetry creates an imbalance that prevents startups (characterized by high information asymmetries) from finding financial resources.

Initial public offering (IPO): The first offering of stock by a company to the public. New public offerings must be registered with the stock market regulator authority. The IPO is one of the methods that a startup can use to raise additional capital for further growth in the late stage.

Invested capital: It is equal to the total amount of capital that has already been invested in portfolio companies.

Investment bank: A type of financial institution, which underwrites new debt and equity securities for corporations, aids in the issue, placement and sale of securities, and helps to facilitate mergers and acquisitions and reorganizations for private and public investors.

Investment memorandum: A sort of "prospectus" that is presented to potential investors of a VC fund. It contains the objectives of the fund, the investment strategy, the curricula of VC managers, the fund cost and the governance structure.

Investment rights agreement: A legal document included in the term sheet and listing any special rights of the investors.

Invoice financing: Consists of the sale of a commercial invoice to a financial intermediary (i.e. a bank) or an online platform in exchange for an interest rate, to support a company's working capital.

Invoice trading = Invoice financing

IPO = Acronym for **Initial public offering**.

IPO prospectus: Document that companies undergoing an IPO are required to file by the market regulatory authority (e.g. the SEC in the US) that provides details about the investment offering to the public.

Keep it all: A crowdfunding model in which the entrepreneur collects all the money raised from the crowd, even if a predetermined threshold, called funding goal, is not reached.

Late phase: The state of a company that has proven its concept, achieved significant revenue compared to its competition and is approaching cash flow breakeven or positive net income. Typically, a later stage company is about 6 to 12 months away from a liquidity exit event, such as IPO or buyout.

Lending-based crowdfunding: A crowdfunding model, in which investors lend money to an individual or a company in exchange for an interest rate and the reimbursement of the capital.

Lifecycle = Company lifecycle

Limited partners (LPs): The investors of a limited partnership VC fund.

Lock-up clause: A clause that prevents a company's prior investors from selling their shares for some lock-up period (usually 6–12 months) that follows the IPO.

M&A = Mergers and Acquisitions = Trade sale

Management fees: A percentage of the committed or invested capital used annually by general partners to cover the fixed costs of managing the fund.

Mergers and Acquisitions (M&A) = Trade sale

Milestone: Key achievements realized by a startup, e.g. the finalization of a prototype, the commercialization of the product.

Minibonds: Medium-/long-term debt securities issued by unlisted startups and small and medium-sized enterprises (SMEs). They can be used for development plans, investments or refinancing operations, allowing startups and SMEs to open up to the public capital market and reducing their dependence on bank loans.

Misappropriation risks: In corporate venture capital, the appropriation of an asset or technology developed by CVC-backed startups, from the CVC parent company for profit.

Moral hazard: It happens when an individual has an incentive to increase her risk exposure as she does not bear the full cost of that risk. For example, an entrepreneur is incentivized to invest the capital borrowed by a bank in riskier projects because she fully benefits from the higher returns of such projects, while the company's limited liability places a lower limit on the losses that would occur in unfavorable conditions.

Multiple analysis = Comparable multiple analysis

Pecking order theory: Since the cost of financing increases with information asymmetries, different sources of capital (internal funds, debt, equity) have different costs. This creates a hierarchy of sources of finance for startups: the preferred source is the internal capital of the entrepreneur, then debt and finally equity capital.

Peer-to-peer business lending (P2P): A crowdfunding model in which investors lend money to a company in exchange for an interest rate and the reimbursement of the capital.

Pitch = Elevator pitch

Post-money valuation: A company's market value after the current investment round; the amount of the investment divided by the ownership percentage offered to the investor.

Pre-money valuation: A company's market value prior to the current investment round; the post-money valuation minus the amount of the investment.

Pre-screening: The preliminary activity of analyzing potential targets of investment, before screening.

Private capital market: Capital provided by private financial intermediaries, such as venture capitalists or business angels.

Proponent: In crowdfunding, those who launch a crowdfunding campaign seeking financing.

Public capital market: The public stock market.

Public subsidies: Capital provided by local, national and supranational governmental institutions.

Relative valuation = Comparable multiple analysis = Multiple analysis

Reward-based crowdfunding: A crowdfunding model, in which backers receive a reward (i.e. a product, a service, a gadget, a simple "thank you") in exchange for the money pledged to the project.

Round = Financing round

Screening: The activity of analyzing potential targets of investment, before performing due diligence, and making an investment decision.

Seed stage: The state of a company where there is just a proof of concept of the product/service and the entrepreneur is in the process of developing it.

Signaling theory: In a transaction between two parties, characterized by high information asymmetries, one party (i.e. the agent/the entrepreneur) can credibly convey information about itself to the other (i.e. the principal/the investor). To be effective, the signal must be costly. In this way, a separating equilibrium is created in the market, where the principal can discern high- vs. low-quality agents.

Social defenses: In CVC investments, a startup, to reduce misappropriation risks, can accept a CVC investment when it is syndicated with a highly reputable IVC.

Soft commitment: An expression of interest, not yet contractually binding, collected from potential investors of a VC fund.

Staging: When VC investments are provided in subsequent tranches upon the reaching of certain milestones (e.g. the development of a patent or a prototype, the reaching of some specific level of sales).

Startup stage: The state of a company where products are mostly in testing, pilot production or just commercialized. The company may be in the process of incorporation or may already be in business.

Startup: A young company founded by one or more entrepreneurs to develop a unique product or service and bring it to market.

Tag-along clauses: A right allowing shareholder A to force B to include A in any sale of shares made by B.

Term sheet: A summary document that describes all key elements of a proposed VC investment (i.e. offering terms, charter, investor rights agreement).

Time defenses: In CVC investments, a startup, to reduce misappropriation risks, can postpone the CVC investment to a later round.

Trade sale: The sale of a company, or a part of a company, to another business.

Unicorn: A company with a pre-money valuation of 1 billion dollars or more.

Valley of death: Initial phases of a startup, during which the company has begun operation, but is not yet generating positive cash flows.

VC = Acronym for **venture capital** and for **venture capitalist**.

VC firm: The legal company that serves as the general partner of a VC fund.

VC fund: The amount of capital used for VC investments. Typically, a VC fund is a limited partnership with a fixed lifetime, where the capital is provided by limited partners and the fund is managed by a VC firm acting as the general partner.

VCs = Acronym for **venture capitalists**.

Venture capital (VC): Capital used by specialized financial intermediaries for investment in startups and private companies with high growth potential and high risk, with the aim of helping these companies grow and gain a financial return.

Venture capitalist (VC): Financial intermediaries who invest in and monitor startups and private companies with high growth potential and high risk, with the aim of helping these companies grow and gain a financial return.

Write-off: A decrease in the reported value of an asset or a company to zero.

Index